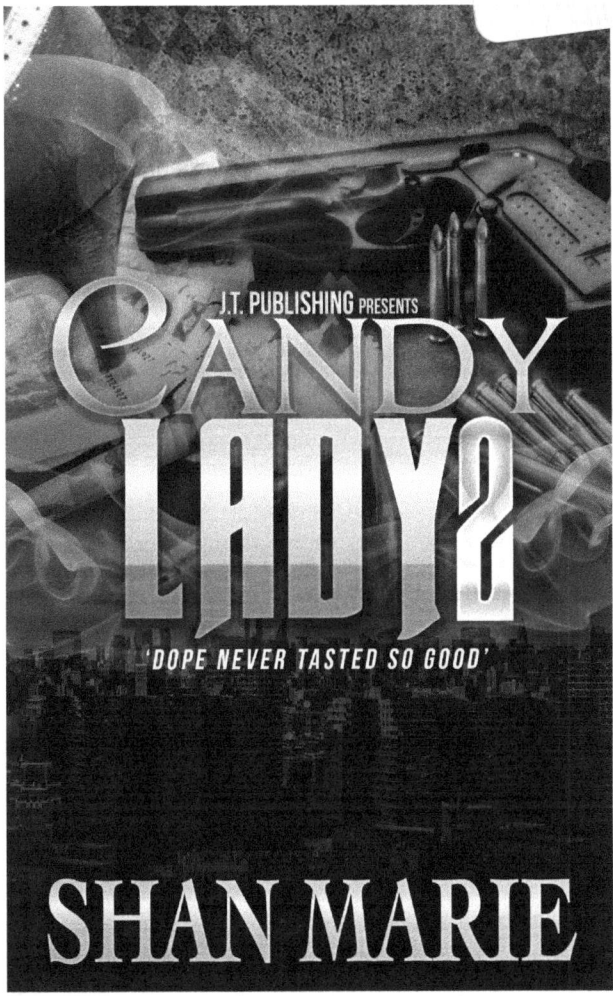

J.T. PUBLISHING PRESENTS

CANDY LADY 2

'DOPE NEVER TASTED SO GOOD'

SHAN MARIE

Published by J.T. Publishing

J.T. Publishing focuses on bringing a reality check to the genre urban literature. All stories are a work of fiction from the authors and are not meant to depict, portray, or represent any particular person Names, characters, places, and incidents are either the product of the author's imagination or are used fictitiously, and any resemblances to an actual person living or dead are entirely coincidental

ISBN: 978-0-9913525-1-7
Edited by: David Good
Layout: Write On Promotions
Cover Design: TSP Creative
Printed in the United States of America

Dedication

I Dedicate This Book to my Nephew, Clayton William Smith (Boogie)!

You are my heart Boogie and Auntie loves you so very much.
If I ever have a son I want him to look up to you as a big cousin and friend.
Right now you're less than a month away from being four years old and I can't imagine my life without you.
That laugh, that smile, those dimples, that charisma; you're a little heartbreaker in the making.
Keep that Capricorn spirit.
Already got some swag about you.
I love you Boogie and always will.

Acknowledgements

My Heavenly Father... Of course I have to first thank my Lord and Savior. God you know me better than I know myself. You love me when I can't, don't and / or won't love myself. I praise you for being God and God alone. Thank You Father for chance after chance. I speak prosperity over my life as a whole, my career as a writer, peace that only You can provide and Joy that the world can't take away from me. This is a dream come true for me, but I know it's nothing for You to Favor and Bless me. Glory to Your Name Father!

#TeamShanMarie...*You B-words Rock*! I now feel that I have a team of wonderful, real, honest, people behind me – pushing me to press on – cheering – shouting it from the mountain top. You chicks are the absolute best and I thank God all the time for each of you. When I was down – you lifted me up – when I felt that I'd never see my name on the cover of a real book – you told me that you could ALREADY see it – when the haters and envious people allowed Satan to use them to try and crash my spirit – you told me to keep my eyes on the prize. I love y'all so much! My circle is small and I like it that way; especially now that the right people are in it! God Bless **#TeamShanMarie**

Kimberly Walker, Atlanta GA... Cuz' I love you like a sister. Thank You for being so supportive and encouraging. Thank You for reading everything I've written. Thank You for the feedback that only you can give in your special way! I love you and appreciate all of the proofreading and critiquing. Forever Dirty Red! Luv Ya! Stay Blessed! **#TeamShanMarie**

Miyako Brogdon, Lithonia GA... MiMi, I never would've thought that you and I would grow in friendship the way that we have. You're missing your calling – *Motivational Speaker Miyako*! I can't count the times that you've brought tears to my eyes with your words of motivation and encouragement. The passion you show for me and my art is unmatchable. You make me feel like the best Urban Street Fiction writer in the world and I love you for that alone. It's like your words have power in them when you're cheering me on – God is good! Be Blessed **#TeamShanMarie**

NaTasha Burks, Tucker GA... Tasha, I cherish the bond we're developing! If I may say so myself, you are the BEST proofreader EVER! (I might have to start paying you a little sumthin, sumthin.) Thank You so much for sharing your time by proofreading for me. Thank You for the support, motivation and encouragement. You have no idea how your words have confirmed that I am doing what I was created to do. Much Luv! God Bless! **#TeamShanMarie**

I'm Blessed To Have You All In My Life -
Walk In the Favor of God,

Shan Marie

CANDY

LADY 2

DOPE NEVER TASTED SO GOOD

PREVIOUSLY IN CANDY LADY (PART 1)...

Kamille 'Kami' Lathan finds herself alone after her long time lover is murdered. She makes it her mission to get her own dope connections and secure a team that she can trust before murdering the man said to be responsible for Carlos' death. She seems to be catching or releasing feelings that were already there for her deceased man's best friend and partner, Joe. Kami decides that she could never treat Carlos in such a disgraceful, wretched way and makes it clear to Joe that nothing will ever happen between them.

In the midst of everything that's going on, Kami can't get her mother off of her mind. She finds out from her incarcerated father that a man by the name of Red may be responsible for her mother's murder.

Against Natacha's advice, Kami brings in an old associate by the name of Bridgette, better known as Bridge. Bridge is a grimy chick, always out for herself and wanting something for nothing. But, she possesses the type of hood-ness Kami needs on her team. At the same time, Natacha adds an old friend to the mix as well; Ronni. Ronni is a simple minded chick, always hustling but never coming up. Kami and Natacha both agree to give the two wanna-be's a chance.

Natacha believes that she may have found Mr.Right in an old fling of hers; she's wrong. Beef gets even tougher between her and Bridge and it begins to cause conflict within the team.

More pressing issues are at hand other than digging up the past of her mother. Kami meets a new drug connection and his partner; Ray and Ace. Things heat up with Natacha and Ace while Kami and Ray take things slow. Kami begins to wonder what Joe's true motives are and if he's really down for her. At this point she can only trust Natacha and that scares her.

Kami's adopted, street child, Tashjma, has become friends with a girl that Kami isn't too fond of. Things seem shady after Tashjma can't be found and Kamille can't help but to think the worst.

Finally, Scotty is dead! Kami has avenged Carlos' murder; killed the nigga that had him killed. Or did she?

1

TASHJMA

"**H**'URRY UP, DALLAS. I'M SUPPOSED TO BE HOME BY NOW." Tashjma is pissed that Dallas is taking her precious time cleaning up. She agreed to meet her at her job, this little burger hut on Cascade, just because she didn't have anything else to do. Truth be told, Tashjma has felt a little lonely being left at home by herself so much lately. But she promised Kamille that she'd be good, besides Kamille always made it up to her.

"I'm coming, damn. These mutha-fuckas don' left grease and shit all over the floor." Dallas never cleans up behind other employees, but she needs to waste a few more minutes until her surprise for Tashjma arrives.

"Shit, I'm finna' go. Kami gon' be home in a minute."

"Damn, you gotta do whatever she tell you to do?"

"Naw, it ain't like that but I told her I wasn't goin' nowhere tonight and she gon' be expecting me to be home."

"Seem like you her lil' slave to me. She treat you like a lil' girl."

"What in the fuck is you talkin' about? Kami took me in, I told you that. She treat me real good and the least I can do is follow the few rules she got. Who you know gon' let you live wit' them and smoke weed wit' them? Nobody. And she don't treat me like no lil' girl, she just want to know where I'm at 'cause she be worried. So you need to shut up about that shit."

"Oh, fuck all that shit you talkin', Tashjma. What? She throw you a few dollars every now and again? I saw that Yukon she picked you up in at school, but I don't see you drivin' it. Nope. That bitch jus' usin' you."

"Usin' me for what? You don't know what the fuck you talkin' about. She throw me more than a few bucks. I get new clothes all the time, my hair stay done and my nails too. I bet you don't make this cleaning them damn floors." Dallas looks over the counter at Tashjma holding a wad of cash. "Shit, Kami take good care of me."

"So the fuck what, bitch." Dallas has jealousy written all over her face.

2

"You the one started the shit. I'm jus' lettin' you know what's up." Tashjma laughs at the expression on Dallas's face. She's not used to having what others don't, so the envy Dallas shows, gives Tashjma contentment.

"Whatever."

"Yeah, whatever." Just then a few taps on the glass door startles Tashjma. "Who the hell is that?"

"Oh, them my folks. Open the door." Dallas orders.

"What's up shawty?" A brown skinned, slim boy speaks through the door as Tashjma stares back at him. There are three guys all together outside the door and Tashjma isn't sure she should open it.

"Open the door, Tashjma." Dallas repeats herself.

Tashjma slowly unlatches the lock and pushes the door open. "Damn girl, what's up wit' that shit?"

"I don't know y'all."

"I know them, Tashjma. I told you them is my folks."

"What's up Dallas?" The short, dark boy speaks while staring at Tashjma.

"Nothin', 'bout to get up out of here."

"You save us somethin' to eat?" The brown skinned boy asks.

"Yep." She slides two big brown bags of food across the counter. "Tashjma, this is my homeboy Derrick." She points to the brown skinned slim guy. "That's Fruit." Again Dallas points, this time to the short dark skinned dude. "And this is my boy, Wayne." There's a cutie sitting at one of the tables in the dining area. Wayne has both eyes on Tashjma and motions for her to come to him.

"What?" She asks, not wanting to approach the young boy.

"Come 'er."

"For what?"

"Damn Dallas, what's up wit' yo girl?" Derrick asks.

"Yeah man, I thought you said she was cool." Fruit throws in his two cents.

"You knew they were coming up here?" Tashjma asks looking over the counter at Dallas.

"Yeah girl, I was tryin' to surprise you."

"Come 'er and get yo present girl." Wayne says with out stretched arms.

"No, I'm good. Matter-of-fact, I'ma go." Tashjma takes a few steps towards the door but is blocked by Derrick.

"Naw, shawty. Dallas said we was all gon' chill. Why you trippin'?"

"I ain't trippin, I just didn't know that y'all was gon' be up here."

4

"Well, you know now, so what's wrong?" Derrick continues.

"Nothin'."

"Alright then, chill, shawty." Tashjma steps back and leans up against the wall. "You want to hit this shit, shawty?" Derrick holds out an 'already rolled' blunt and Tashjma begins to reach. Then she remembers Kamille's words, *'don't smoke behind niggas you don't know. If you ain't seen the shit being rolled up, don't fuck with it,'* so she declines.

"Naw, I'm straight."

"Damn, Tashjma. Any other time you smokin' like a fuckin' chimney." Dallas is pissed that her friend is being rude to her friends.

"It ain't that, I just ... Dallas let me talk to you." Tashjma goes behind the counter and begins to whisper to her friend. "What you tell them dudes I was gon' do with them Dallas?"

"Derrick asked me if I had a friend that one of his boys could holla at and I said yeah. I knew you was gon' trip so that's why I didn't say nothin'."

"I wish you had told me."

"Just chill out and have fun."

"I need to call Kami."

"Damn, Tashjma, you a sucka for that bitch."

"Watch ya mouth Dallas. Don't disrespect her like that. What the fuck is it with you anyway? She ain't don' shit to you."

"You don't know what she...... you know what, fuck it. Let's just chill."

"Yeah, you need to chill."

"Let's just drop the shit, Tashjma."

"Whatever. I'm out."

"Why?"

"'Cause I don't like this shit and plus you is really trippin'."

"Tashjma come on, stay and chill with us."

"Naw, that's alright, I'm good."

"Fuck you then."

"Naw, shawty, fuck you."

Tashjma exits the restaurant in full speed, knowing that she has quite a walk ahead of her. She's trying to figure out what she saw in Dallas as a friend anyway. She's always seemed jealous of her and she talks really negative about Kamille all of the time.

"Hello."

"Kami."

"Yeah, girl where are you?" Kamille has been worried as hell but hadn't called Tashjma because she doesn't want to treat her like a child. She bought her a cell phone and she knows that

Tashjma knows how to use it, so she calmed herself and said that everything would be okay.

"I'm off of Simpson, by the burger place you don't like. Can you come and get me?"

"Yeah, you alright?"

"Yeah. I'll tell you about it when you get here."

"Alright, where are you going to be?"

"That gas station by the grocery store. You know the one I'm talking about?""Yeah, I'm on the way." Kamille has already made it to her SUV and popped the locks. The station that Tashjma is referring to is only about five minutes up the road.

"Aay, shawty, why you leave like that?" Tashjma turns to see the three guys from Dallas' job riding in a car beside her. She doesn't respond and keeps walking towards her destination. "Got-damn, shawty. Why you gotta act like that?" Derrick is growing angrier by the minute. "We was just trying to chill wit' yo stank ass."

"Stupid bitch." Fruit yells from the back seat.

"Fuck y'all niggas. What the fuck do y'all want anyway?" Tashjma speaks as she treads down the sidewalk, only a block from the highly lit gas station.

"We want you, baby." Wayne plays the good guy. "Don't pay no attention to these fools. Won't you stop walkin' so we can talk?"

"Naw, I'm good."

"Man fuck this shit, grab that bitch." Derrick yells as he speeds the car up and turns in front of Tashjma, jumping the sidewalk and slamming on the brakes.

"Y'all niggas is crazy." Tashjma is scared out of her mind but has a sense of relief when she sees Kamille's truck pull into the station.

"Kami!" She yells as Wayne jumps out the front passenger seat. Fruit throws the back door open and pulls on Tashjma as Wayne pushes her into the car. "Let me go, mutha-fucka." She screams to the top of her lungs while throwing punches and kicks at the boys to no avail. Fruit throws a punch that almost knocks her out.

"Shut the fuck up, bitch!" He punches again. This time she feels herself blacking out.

Tashjma presses talk twice on her cell phone to call Kamille again.

"Girl, where are you?" Kamille speaks through her phone.

"What y'all want?" Tashjma cries.

"What?" Kamille is confused.

"It stinks in this old ass Regal."

"Old Regal?" Kamille begins looking around the station and onto the street. She sees a dark blue Regal turning up Simpson Road.

"Tashjma, what's up? Are you alright?" Kamille speaks through the phone again with no direct response.

"What y'all gon' do to me?"

"Shut the fuck up, bitch. Befo' I shut you the fuck up." Fruit is by far the most violent.

Kamille throws the car into drive and punches the petal. Catching up to the old Regal she slows, she doesn't want to draw any attention to herself. She can see Tashjma sitting in the back seat. She doesn't want to hang up from her so she presses talk to use the three-way feature on her cell phone. *"Coupe, where you at?"*

"Off of Simpson about to dump this damn grimlin, what's up?

"I knew your ass was over here. Look, some dudes got Tashjma, I don't know what's going on but I'm behind them, I need you to catch up to me."

"Where you at?"

"On Simpson, passing that Chinese place you like to eat at. I'm headed up towards Lee Street."

"Oh shit, I'm two minutes away. You in the Yukon right?"

"Yeah. They're in a blue Regal."

"Alright."

Tashjma turns slightly to look out the back window and sees Kamille trailing closely. "Man, I ain't got nothin' for y'all." Of course, Tashjma has stopped crying now that she knows that Kamille will save her from these fake ass thugs.

"Oh, you got it shawty. And we gon' get it."

"What's up though? Dallas put y'all up to this?"

"You askin' too many fuckin' questions." Derrick speaks from the drivers' seat. "Aay, find that dough, Fruit." Fruit begins to feel all over Tashjma pulling at her jean and jacket pockets. .

"What dough? Stop nigga!" Tashjma punches Fruit in the head a few times and he grabs her arm. Smack! Smack!

He slaps her twice and she lays still. All of a sudden her tears return. "Bitch!" He yells as he takes both hands and begins to choke her.

"Don't kill her in here." Derrick says from the driver's seat.

Fruit releases his grip. "Kill me?" Tashjma says while gasping for breath. "Y'all gon' kill me?"

"Don't worry, we gon' have a lil' fun wit' ya first." Derrick replies, assuring Tashjma that they are planning to kill her.

"Y'all serious about that shit?" Wayne finally says something. He's been thinking about this situation and regrets being a part of it.

"Hell yeah nigga, we gon' do this shit right now."

"Man, I thought we were just gon' have some fun."

"This *is* fun!"

Tashjma sits up in the seat trying to catch her breath and composure. She turns again to be sure that Kamille is still there; she is. She looks out the window to the right and sees an old Buick and realizes that she knows the guy. She can't think of his name but she knows that she's seen him at Kamille's house several times.

The old Buick speeds up and jumps in front of the Regal. "What the fuck!" Derrick yells at the rude driver of the other car. "Learn how to drive mutha-fucka." He continues.

Suddenly, a black Suburban pulls up on the right side and that driver looks familiar to Tashjma also. The Buick breaks his speed massively causing Derrick to slow. He's aggravated and tries to get over but the Suburban is riding right beside them. Tashjma turns to look at Kamille again and she's right on their tail now. Tashjma smiles and crosses her legs in confidence.

"What in the fuck is everybody doing?" Derrick hasn't noticed the setup. "Why in the fuck is that truck on my ass?"

They all turn to look at Kamille and she puts her bright lights on them. "Damn! What the fuck?" Fruit whines.

Kamille waits until there's hardly any traffic around and makes the call to Coupe. *"Whenever you're ready, Coupe."*

"Cool." Coupe slams on the brakes of the old Buick causing the Regal to slam into the back. He then takes off and breaks his speed again, still in front of the regal.

"Got-damn!" Derrick smashes into the steering wheel and Wayne's head slams into the front windshield.

"Fuck! I'm fuckin' bleeding." Wayne cries out.

The Suburban rams the old Regal from the side, forcing it off the road. Kamille reluctantly rams her Yukon into the back of the Regal over and over again. She just bought the damn thing and doesn't want to have to buy another one. However, she must save Tashjma from whatever she's gotten herself into.

"Got-damn! What the fuck is going on?" Fruit looks over at Tashjma as the car is being bounced around.

12

"Y'all better let me the fuck out of here. Stupid mutha-fuckas. Y'all didn't know who the fuck y'all was messin' wit'."

"What, bitch?" Derrick yells. "You did this shit?"

"Y'all mutha-fuckas in trouble, that's all I know." Fruit jumps over on Tashjma, punching her in the face, chest and stomach over and over again.

Kamille can see that Tashjma is in trouble and rams the car again, this time knocking it into Coupe. Coupe hits the breaks, attempting to stop the Regal and he does. The Suburban stops on the side of it and Traz climbs across the seat and hops out the passenger side. Coupe jumps out the Buick and Kamille slowly steps out of the Yukon. Derrick, Fruit and Wayne frantically look around. Kamille walks up to Fruit's door and opens it with her .45 aimed at his head. The other side of the car is mangled and no one can get in or out, plus Traz has them blocked in. "Get out." She orders Fruit.

"Aay man, what the fuck is this?" Derrick yells from the front with blood running down his face.

Traz places a quick shot to his head. "Shut the fuck up."

"Oh shit, don't kill me please." Wayne begs.

Fruit falls out of the car onto his face and cries out. "We was just bull shittin' man."

Kamille looks in the car at Tashjma. "Come on." She motions for her to get out of the car and she does. "You alright?" Kamille asks while touching Tashjma's face full of bruises.

"Yeah, I guess."

"Drive the truck." Kamille points to the Yukon and Tashjma gladly runs to the driver's side and hops in.

"Get rid' of 'em." Kamille makes the order and Coupe shoots Wayne twice in the chest while Fruit tries to run. Traz catches up with him and shoots him four times in the back. There are a few people across the street in a parking lot getting ready to enter a sports bar. When they hear the shots they all hit the pavement. On this side of town, the sound is very familiar and folks already know what to do. Coupe and Traz quickly put Fruit back into the car and move Derrick over. Traz hops in the driver's seat while Kamille jumps into the old Buick and takes off. Coupe follows in his Suburban with Tashjma right behind him.

2

TASHJMA

"KAMI, WHAT'S UP?"

"Who is this?"

"Nard."
"Hey Nard, what's up baby?"
"Shit. It's a chick been asking about you."
"Who?"
"I don't know her. She's a friend of a dude I deal with down in Florida."

Instantly, the female that Sylvester told her about comes to mind. *"Have you seen her?"*

"Yeah, she light skinned, tall, slim, nice looking chick."

"*Older?*"

"*Yeah, you know her?*"

"*Naw, but someone told me a while ago that she needed the hook-up.*"

"*Yeah, she said she heard about you and wanted to do some business with you.*"

"Is s*he in the 'A'?*"

"*Yep.*"

"*Alright, hook it up and get back at me.*"

"*Shit, they over here now, Kami.*"

"*Alright, I'll come through then.*"

Kamille arrives at Bernard's house in less than thirty minutes, anxious to meet Jackie. Not because she needs the business but simply because she intrigues her. How can a woman of her age be so stupid? There's no way in the hell Kamille would live out in the open like that, not in her line of business. The photos that were shown to her by Pepper let Kamille know a lot about this Jackie woman. One, she doesn't care about getting caught by the FEDS. Two, she's hot tempered and three she's a little too sensual in public.

"What's up, y'all?" Kamille enters the basement door reluctantly.

"Yo', Kami." Bernard greets her and motions for her to have a seat. "This is Blake and Jackie."

"Hey, how are y'all?"

"Alright." Blake is the first to speak.

"I hear you've been looking for me." Kamille directs her statement towards Jackie but there seems to be something else on her mind. "You want to do business?" Kamille looks into Jackie's face and waits for a response.

"Jackie." Blake, a short needle of a man, nudges her back into reality.

"Yeah."

"Is something wrong?" Kamille is a little spooked out by Jackie's behavior.

"No, I'm just a little taken back by how young you are."

"Oh, okay." Kamille directs her attention towards Bernard. "So Nard, I assume you've searched them already?"

"Fo' sho', Kami." Bernard isn't offended by the question, strictly business. "No wires; just a .45 on Jackie and a Beretta on Blake."

"What do you need?" Back to Jackie.

"Thirty or forty kilos."

"Okay, give me a number and I'll have someone hook up with you sometime this evening."

"If you don't mind, I'd like to deal directly with you."

"I can't do that."

"Why not?"

"You should know how it works Jackie. I can't put my hands in it like that. I have people that handle that for me." The only times Kamille has actually had that amount of drugs in her possession is when she made her first and second buy from Ace and Ray. That was only because she needed to meet them and handle her deal. Other than that, the head of the clan, which is Kamille, should never be in direct contact.

"I can appreciate that but I want to talk to you and get to understand your way of working."

"What do you want to know?"

Jackie looks around the room, glaring at Bernard and Blake. "Can we take a walk?"

Kamille thinks for a second, "yeah, that's cool."

The women walk down the street quiet at first, feeling each other out. "Kami!" A male voice yells out. Kamille turns in the direction of the call and throws her hand in the air to say hello.

"What is Kami short for?" Jackie breaks the silence with a question that is intended to begin the small talk.

"Kamille."

"Oh, okay. Are you from here?"

"Born and raised."

"Cool."

"So what's up, Jackie?"

"I'd just rather deal with the head bitch in charge, you know? We're in the same boat. We both have moves to make and not a lot of time to waste."

"True, but that's not how I operate. Like I said, I can hook you up with one of my employees and they'll happily place your orders with me."

"If that's how it has to be done, that's fine."

"How'd you hear about me anyway?"

"Your name carries a lot of weight. Everybody who's anybody knows about you by now. My old connect got killed so I need a new one."

"Who was that?"

"Scotty."

Kamille isn't surprised. 'Yeah, he got messed up."

"Yep." Jackie looks at Kamille with a suspicious eye.

"What?"

"I hear you fucked him up."

"Where'd you hear that?"

"Just from around the way."

"Naw."

Jackie gives a disbelieving stare. "Really?"

"Yep, really."

"So what happened to your ol' man?"

"He got messed up too."

"By who?"

Something in Jackie pulls Kamille to her. She has an instant trust in her and that has never happened before. "Scotty."

"What? Why?"

"I don't know."

"That's fucked up." Jackie knows now that Kamille killed Scotty. If she's anything like she thinks, she had to kill him.

"Are you going to be in town tomorrow?"

"Yeah, I'll be here for a few days."

"Take a ride with me tomorrow then."

"Alright."

3

THE LADIES DECIDE TO PAY **QUINC A VISIT..** They just knew that he'd come on board with the plan. Although Quinc and Carlos got along well, Quinc has always been a rock-headed dude. Always looking for a 'come-up', no matter from who or how he gets it. He's the jealous type, stubborn and quick to pull the trigger.

"Hell naw. What the fuck? You thank you just gon' come and take over?" Quinc seems to be upset that Kamille has taken her rightful place in this 'game' of drugs and murder.

"I've already taken over, Quinc. You were buying from Los anyway, so what's the problem?"

"That's different."

"I see. You'd shop with Los, but not me."

"Damn right. Shit, now that Scotty ain't around, I'll have to find a new connect. But, I'll be straight for a minute."

"Alright. You know you have to move off my blocks, don't you?"

"Yo' blocks?"

"Do you think this is a joke, Quinc?" Her voice is serene and her heartbeat has yet to speed up.

Quinc pulls out his 'tool', pointing it directly at Kamille. Concurrently, his boys, Natacha, Ronni and Jackie 'pull out' as well. Kamille sits across from Quinc with the most placid look on her face; legs crossed, arms resting on the table.

"I ain't moving shit!" He's yelling and two big veins are popping in the middle of his forehead.

"You *will* move." Jackie has to allow a slight grin to ease across her face when Kamille says this. She's standing to the left of Kamille, anxious and waiting to prove that she is worthy to be in the presence of the 'great' Kami. She's pleased at how Kamille is handling business and has to wonder who taught her to operate the way that she does.

"You want to go to war with me, Kami? You talkin' a lot of shit." Kamille is silent, starring into his eyes, not blinking once. "You think I'm scared of you?"

"The question is do you want to die right here?"

"What?" Silence. Kamille knows that he heard her question, so there's no need to repeat her self. "Alright, you lucky you was Los' girl." Quinc puts his gun back in his pants and his boys lower their arms. "You gon' tell yo' girls to put they 'tools' up?"

"Rule number two?" She asks and Quinc is confused. Although Kamille is still starring him in the eyes, the question is not directed towards him.

Natacha responds, still with her 'tool' raised. "Never pull it, unless you gon' use it." Bang! Natacha lets out one quick shot and shoots Quinc square in the middle of his forehead, releasing the pressure from those veins.

Kamille comes up quick, pulling her .45 from her waist. The ladies and gentlemen exchange gunfire in a civil war that lasts all of two minutes. Maybe Quinc would have done business with Kamille and not have caused any trouble. But it's too late. He should've never tried her like that. If he's acting a fool now, there's a good chance that he'll act a fool later. With Quinc and his boys laid out, the ladies nonchalantly gather all the money, drugs and guns that the breathless gentlemen will no longer need.

Quinc ran most of east Atlanta. The guys that he had running his shops were faithful associates of Carlos and Kamille didn't have any trouble with them falling in line. Now, it's time for the ladies to pay a visit to Ethan. Ethan is Red's son. The man responsible for Victoria's murder. Kamille will have to get rid of him but for the time being, she'll let him live. This is a top-notch nigga with his whole life embedded into the game. Ethan and Carlos have had words in the past but Scotty put an end to it. He told them that since both of them worked for him, they'd have to keep it cool. They did, for the most part. They stayed away from each other as much as possible.

"What's up, Ethan?" Kamille stands leaning against the building while Natacha, Ronni and Jackie make conversation with the other 'dope boys'.

"Shit Kami, what you know, good girl?"

"Everything's lovely."

"I hear. So who's this?" Ethan is looking at Jackie. Her bright red complexion and long legs have him in a daze.

"This is Jackie."

"What's up?" Jackie returns the hello with a nod. With his attention back on Kamille, Ethan asks, "I guess you're here to see where I stand?"

"Yeah."

24

"I'm not sure yet. You know me and Los weren't too cool, but I ain't never had a problem wit' you. I been thinking about it and the only way I'll deal is if I can take College Park too." Now Ethan is already over East Point. All the dope that flows through there comes from him. The two cities sit right next to each other and many people can't distinguish between the two.

"How big are you shopping?"

"I need a good bit right now; at least fifteen bricks, 'X' pills and heavy on the 'green'; at least ten pounds."

"You can have College Park." Ethan looks surprised at the response he just received. Kamille has had enough killing for the past few days to last a lifetime, so he's caught her at a good time. She'll appease him for now. As long as he shops with her, there's no problem. The money rotates and Kamille can easily move her guys around if need be. "You got folks to put in or you want to keep my peeps?"

"You can take everyone but Spook. The nigga do good work and I'd like to have him." The dope game is just like a legitimate business. Employees can be shifted around and even relocated as needed. It's just up to the head ladies and gentlemen in charge. If an employee wants to keep a shop, he or she must relocate if told to.

"I just gave him another shop off Godby Road, so that's cool. But his other shop is on the Westside and that's me all the way. I can put someone else in but when he comes to you, he's going to want to still have two shops. But that'll be up to you, of course."

"Ummm. I don't know, I have a lot of folks I gotta make sure everyone eats, you know."

"I feel ya."

"See you got bigger turf, so you can give a nigga more than one shop and everything stays cool."

"True. But like I said, you're in charge of it now, so it's your call."

"Yeah, I want 'em around, so I'll probably give 'em two, but the other workers gon' be jealous."

"I'll let him know tonight and the trade begins as soon as you shop wit' me."

"I'm ready. You got the goods?"

"Oh yeah. Let's head in." The two make their way into the shop as Kamille gives Natacha a 'get the shit' nod.

Ethan takes his finger and pokes it into the sample bag Kamille brought along and then takes a sniff and a lick of his finger. "Damn Kami, who you shoppin' wit', some niggas out the country or somethin'?"

"It's some good shit, isn't it?" Natacha asks as she walks into the room with a duffle bag full of dope.

"Hell yeah."

"So what do you need, E?"

"Gimme twenty of that shit, ten bags of 'X' and ten of the 'green'." Ethan seems very excited about the new product and plans on finding out where Kamille shops. "Listen, Kami. I got this cousin up in Detroit that's having a hard time getting a connect. Do you think you can holla at 'em??"

"Yeah, I can do that. When do you want to ride up?"

"Soon as possible."

"Alright, I'll be in touch."

Kamille walks into Tashjma's room and sits on the bed next to her. "What's up?"

"Nothing." Tashjma answers with her head down.

"What happened, Tashjma?" Kamille doesn't feel the need to beat around the bush.

"You ain't been wanting to know." Tashjma gets up from the bed and walks over to the dresser, pretending to look for something.

"What?"

"You been too busy to ask about what happened that night, Kami. So why now?" She's been upset for the last day or so but Kamille hasn't been home to notice.

"Are you implying that I don't care?" Kamille can't believe the audacity this girl has. She's just had three boys killed for her and if anyone else was involved they'll certainly die also. Kamille doesn't like killing kids, even though she didn't pull the trigger, she's still responsible. Derrick, Wayne and Fruit got what they deserved. They were gonna kill Tashjma, so Kamille had to protect her.

"I know you care."

"Then what the fuck are you talking about Tashjma? Why are you being a brat all of a sudden? Yeah, I've been gone but I have to handle my business or else the shit will fall apart. Now, I'm sorry that I haven't been able to be here for you but, if you recall, I was there when those dudes had you in their car."

"You sure were, Kami. I'm sorry. My mind is just a little messed up."

"Talk to me. What's up?"

"Okay, I went up to Dallas's job because she asked me to."

"I knew that lil' girl was involved."

"How'd you know?"

"I just knew, plus she's fake as hell."

"Why you say that?"

"Tashjma, you haven't hung around females consistently. Hoes are shady. When you find one that's cool as a fucking fan, then you'll know and that's a rare occasion. The rest are all the same. They talk too much and keep a lot of mess going."

"Someone cool like Natacha."

"Yeah, but the majority of females are worthless when it comes to true friendship. Anyway, go ahead with what you were saying."

"Well she had pissed me off 'cause she always wants to talk about you and..."

Kamille must interrupt. "Me? What? That chick doesn't even know me."

"I know. That's what I told her. She kept talkin' about you don't take care about me and stuff like that. Which I knew the chick was being jealous, so I pulled out my wad of cash and showed the bitch. So all of a sudden those dudes show up and they want to smoke. Plus, I know they wanted to screw too. So me and Dallas had some more words and I left. After I called you to come pick me up, them dudes rode up on me and threw me in the car. They said they were gonna have some fun with me before they killed me. I asked if Dallas put them up to it and they wouldn't say."

"Do you think she did?"

"I don't know." Frustration shows on Tashjma's face. She's never had any true friends and it hurts that things aren't working out with Dallas.

"From what you've told me, she did. Why in the hell would they roll up on you like that? It doesn't make since unless she sent them after you."

"They knew about the money that I had on me. One of them said to search me for the dough and that's when the guy in the back started feeling on me."

"So if they weren't there when you showed Dallas the money, you know that she had to tell them that, right?"

"Yeah, I guess so."

"You guess so?" Kamille is becoming more and more aggravated with Tashjma's ignorance. She tells herself that the youngster doesn't understand what's really going on and lets it go.

"Like what?"

"You're family with people that revenge is second nature to, meaning that if you want to 'get' Dallas, we can 'get' her."

"You think we should?"

"Evidently the hoe wants you for some unknown reason. But it's up to you."

"What would you do?"

Kamille gives a 'you know damn well what I would do' look. "I'll be honest, Tashjma. I don't like the girl. But like I said, it's up to you."

"Ummm. I don't know but I don't think that I want to kill her." She whispers the last comment because she can't believe that she's actually having a conversation about killing someone. Not that she cares about Dallas like that, but she never thought that she'd have the say so over such a thing.

"I won't force you to pull the trigger, Tashjma. This 'game' is full of murder and tough decisions. There's no way that I'd force you into this. That's the main reason that I don't know if you should be living with me."

"I don't want to live anywhere else, Kami." Tears begin to flow down Tashjma's face. Please don't make me leave."

"I'm not saying that you have to leave right now but this is something that you really need to think about. As long as I'm looking out for you and stuff like this happens there will be more deaths like the other night. This is what I do and right now, it's my only option."

"Okay, I understand. Can I think about the situation with Dallas before I decide?"

"Alright, watch your back." Kamille won't push the subject but she has to be sure that Tashjma is okay. If she doesn't want Dallas taken 'out', then she won't be taken 'out'. However, if push comes to shove, she'll be forced to make the decision herself.

4

BRIDGE

"**W**HERE YOU BEEN, MA'?" Joe pulls Bridgett to him.

"Nowhere."

"Shit, you been somewhere. Where were you last night?"

"Chillin' with Kami."

"Don't lie to me." He grabs her wrist while giving her a look that should very well scare her.

"I'm not." She pulls away not realizing how serious he's being right now.

"Look bitch, I ain't got time for yo' games. Something's going on 'cause Kami hit Quinc and his boys last night."

"How do you know Kami did it?"

"I just know. I've been doing this a long fuckin' time, alright!"

"Well, I don't know nothin' about no Quinc."

"What do you know?" He grabs her again, but this time with more force not allowing her to break free.

"Nigga, you betta let me go! What the fuck is wrong with you?"

"Ain't shit wrong with me, yo'. You gon' tell me what the fuck's been up the last few nights or do I have to beat it out of you?"

"Beat me? Please, you need to let me go before I fuck you up."

Smack! Joe pimp slaps her knocking her to the floor. "Get the fuck up!" He kicks Bridgett like he's kicking a football trying to score those extra points. "You a loud mouthed bitch. You must not know who the fuck I am." He kicks her again even harder, directly into her rib cage. "Get the fuck up!" He yells, kicking her again.

"Okay!" Bridgett cries as she pulls herself off the floor trying massively to catch her breath.

"Now what?"

"I just stayed at Kami's house to handle some business the other night, that's all. I don't know anything about last night or Quinc."

"What business?"

"I don't even know what it was all about. They left me at the house."

Joe knows that she's lying. "You think I fuck you for the hell of it? You ain't shit to me! You need to know what the fuck is going on over there."

"So that's it? You fuck me for information? Why don't you just ask Kami what's up?"

"Don't worry about that. I know you know more than you're saying too."

"I don't know shit." Smack! Another slap. "Stop hitting me, mutha-fucka." Bridgett tries to attack Joe but fails. Her attempts are followed by more slaps and even more brutal punches to the face and stomach.

"You think you can whoop me, bitch? Huh? You think I won't kill yo' motherfuckin' ass right here? Huh?"

"Do it nigga and you'll have Kami on yo' ass."

Smack! Smack! "Who in the fuck do you think I am? I run this shit."

"Alright." She cries out with her hands shielding her face.

"Say it."

"Say what?"

"Tell me who runs this shit."

"You do."

"What?"

35

"You run this."

"You got-damn right! Now get up and go clean off yo' fuckin' face."

"What happened to you?" Kamille opens her door to find Bridgett looking like she's been hit by a bus.

"Joe."

"I told yo' ass."

"I don't need no shit right now Kami."

"Alright. What do you want me to do?"

"Nothin'."

"Come on and get cleaned up." Bridgett follows Kamille to the hall bathroom.

"Why you got all your stuff in boxes already? You moving now?"

"Yep."

"Where to?"

"I don't know yet."

"Why you movin'?"

"I just need a new scene. You know things aren't the same since Los died. I have to get out of here."

"So you expect me to believe that you just decided to move and you don't know where you're goin'?"

"It's the truth." Kamille grabs a hand towel and tries to clean some of the dried blood from Bridgett's face.

"That's bullshit."

"What the fuck is wrong with you?" Kamille can't believe the nerve of this ungrateful female.

"You bullshittin' me, that's what's wrong."

"So what?"

"Why though?"

"Because it's not any of your business. When I'm ready for you to know where I am, I'll tell you." Kamille is trying to remain calm.

"What?" Bridgett is offended.

"You heard me. I'm tryin' to clean yo' motherfuckin' ass up and you sittin' here talking all this shit. Let that nigga try and get those bruises down." Kamille throws the towel in Bridgett's face.

"Fuck you, Kami. You ain't never been down for nobody but yo' damn self."

"You're a lie! I was there when the last nigga whooped yo' ass. I got yo' sorry ass somewhere to live and this is the bullshit you bring to me? I told yo' dumb ass not to fuck with Joe in the first place, but you wanted to get fucked. Now look at 'cha." Kamille is tired of coming to Bridgett's rescue and getting nothing but lip for it. "Bitch, you betta get yo' ass out of my house right now."

"I told you that bitch ain't shit." Natacha speaks from the other end of the phone.

37

"*I know, but I was trying to give her the benefit of the doubt.*"

"*Forget that trick. Ain't no telling what the hell she's been telling Joe.*"

"*I know. Let's ride down to his shop and see how his business is going.*"

"*Alrigh.; I'll be there in ten minutes.*"

5

"CAN I GO WITH YOU, KAMI?"

Tashjma startles Kamille.

"Damn girl, announce yourself!"

"Sorry." Kamille has been on edge every since Carlos was murdered, but lately things have been becoming more and more intense.

"Yeah, you have to go because the moving men are on the way."

"They gon' move all yo' stuff?"

"Yeah. By the time we get back from running around, they should be finished." There's a knock at the door and Tashjma takes off running to answer it. "Hold on, shawty. You don't know who that is at the door." Kamille pushes the peephole cover to the side and sees Jackie standing there. She opens the door, shocked that Jackie has popped up at her house.

"Hey, Kami."

"What's up?"

"Just wanted to see if we could hang today?"

Kamille can't help but to feel a sense of comfort around Jackie. She's tried to shake it but there's no use. She likes the old woman. "Yeah, that's cool. Natacha is on her way to get me now."

"Where are y'all going?"

"I need to check on a few shops and handle some business, you know the routine."

"All too well."

The four ladies ride in Natacha's Jeep to pay Joe a visit.

"Tashjma, wait in the car."

"I know." She whines.

"What's up, Joe?"

"Damn, Ma'. I been tryin' to reach you." Joe gets up from his seat.

"What's up?" Kamille keeps her distance. She's never been the one to walk around a crack house.

"Not much."

"I thought you said business had slacked? Everything looks booming to me."

"Yeah, it just picked back up."

"Hum." Kamille looks Joe in his eyes.

"What's that, Ma'?"

"Nothing, just thinking."

"About what?"

"Business, that's all."

"Alright. You don' any business with that dude Ace?"

"Just what we did the night at the restaurant." Kamille keeps her dealings to minimum ears. She likes it that way. "Why? You need to re-up?"

"Naw, I'm straight?"

"That's just it, Joe." Enough is enough. "How is it that you hardly ever have to re-up but your shop is packed like this?"

Joe looks over at Jackie standing next to Natacha listening to every word. He's uncomfortable with discussing his personal affairs. "These mutha-fuckas don't shop that good, that's all. They be nickel and dimming my ass."

"Hum." Kamille looks around at the house full of junkies, all chilling and doing their dope. Some are clutched up in corners others finding a place on a wall, watching all of the other fiends to be sure that no one is attempting to rob them of their goods. "Alright, we're just making rounds."

"You never checked on me before, why now?"

"I'll be checking from now on, just so I know first hand what's up."

Joe stares at Kamille with unevenness of what she's really looking for. "Alright. I'll walk with y'all outside."

"Alright."

Joe follows the ladies out of the shop making small talk along the way.

"I see you didn't waste any time with Bridge." Natacha states.

Joe pauses with a distant look on his face and then realizes that the cat is out of the bag. "Pussy is pussy." He states shrugging his shoulders.

"Yeah, to some niggas." She responds, rolling her eyes.

Joe attempts to ignore Natacha and diverts his attention towards Kamille. "So Kami, I guess any chance of us is over huh?"

"It never started Joe. There wasn't a slight chance before but there's absolutely none now."

"'Cause I fucked Bridge? That hoe came on to me yo'."

"It doesn't matter and it's no lost, with either one of you."

"Damn Kami, it's like that?"

"Has to be."

"Alright. So when were you gonna fill me in on Scotty?" Joe asks, now filling that he has turned the tables.

"What do you want to know?"

"Everything, Ma'. Shit, you making moves that I was supposed to be in on, but you ain't said shit to me."

"You have your secrets and I have mine."

"Secrets? What secrets? You know me better than that." Kamille lets out a slight smirk. "Damn ma', what's really good?"

"Nothing, Joe."

"What about Quinc?"

"What about him?"

"What happened?"

"He didn't want to join the team and things got ugly. You know how that goes right? Niggas *say* they are a part of the team but they have their own shit going down on the side. You understand, right?" She stares Joe in the eyes again.

He brushes off the feeling that she knows about his side deals. How could she? He was there when she met Ace and they didn't talk long enough for him to mention Joe, so he thinks. "I would've gone with you to see about Quinc. Why didn't you call me?" He asks, ignoring her eye contact.

"I took care of it."

"You and who?"

"Why so many questions?" Kamille is becoming aggravated.

43

"I just want to know what's up. Damn, a lil' while ago you had me filled in on everything. Now, I gotta beg information out of you. I know you didn't take that crazy ass Bridge with you." Joe wants to be sure that Bridgett wasn't lying to him.

"Business was handled. That should be the only concern, right?"

"Naw, Ma'. That ain't it." Joe is becoming angry.

"That's all you need to know."

"What the fuck, Kami? You treating me like shit right now. Like I ain't been here from the beginning. You treatin' me foul yo'."

"No, I'm not. There are certain things that need to stay on the low."

"You keeping shit from me and that ain't cool, Ma'."

"A lot of shit ain't been cool lately."

"Look, Ma'. You need me with you. I thought that's what we discussed. I know you didn't take that junky ass Ronni with you."

"Junky? Ronni's not a junky."

"Shit, Ma'. This is what I'm talking about. That fuckin' Ronni got her nose deep in that shit."

"How do you know this?"

"Spook filled me in on her ass weeks ago." Joe is trying to get back in good with Kamille. Even though he doesn't know how he got on her bad side to begin with.

"Why didn't you mention it to me?"

"I figured you knew. Shit, you got everything so tight." Kamille can hear the sarcasm as Joe lets a 'joker' grin smear his face.

"Cute." The ladies exit Joe's presence.

Back in the car, the ladies speak on the subject of Ronni.

"You think she's doing powder for real?" Natacha asks.

"I don't know. If she is, the bitch is out. Come to think about it, that bitch was high as hell at my party that night. Too high. Shit, we got too much going on to have cloudy heads and shit."

"Who is that guy?" Tashjma asks.

"Joe." Natacha answers.

"I've seen him before."

"Where?" Kamille asks.

"He came to Deloris house."

"Who in the fuck is Deloris?" Natacha asks still pissed at the thought of Ronni stuffing 'powder' up her nose.

"The big, butch, bitch from the club." Kamille answers.

"Mutha-fucka." Natacha is piecing everything together.

"He has been sending all these folks after me."

"He the one told Deloris them to try and beat you up, Kami?" Tashjma asks.

"Gotta be. Ain't no other explanation for this shit."

"Wait." Jackie is confused. "What in the hell is going on? I thought that was your boy."

"He was, but I don't know now." Kamille answers. "We grew up together and he was my ol' man's right hand."

"When them niggas came to get Los, did they say Scotty sent them?" Natacha asks.

"Yeah and so did the dykes at the club. This mutha-fucka got a hit out on me and telling these goons to say Scotty's name. Ain't that a bitch?"

"So we killed Scotty for nothing. He was telling the truth."

"He had to go anyway. In order for us to take over, Scotty had to go. But got-damn, this nigga all in my shit and coming around me like he's on my side."

"That's why you wanted to keep him out of yo' business."

"Hell yeah, something just wasn't sitting right with him."

"How many times did he come over to Deloris house?" Natacha asks Tashjma.

"Twice while I was there. They went into the bedroom and talked, then he left."

"Did he see you?"

"Yeah."

"So now what, Kami?" Natacha asks.

"I don't know, but this nigga wants my life and I want his. So we have to move quickly."

6

NATACHA & FELIX

"*THIS WAS NICE.*"

Natacha snuggles under Felix as they walk through The Melting Pot's parking lot.

"Yeah it was."

"You want to go back to my place and relax?"

"You know the answer to that." He kisses her softly on the lips.

Just as Felix opens Natacha's door and lets her in the car a strange man walks up to him. "Hey mister, you got a dollar?" Felix is shocked that there would be panhandlers in this area but Natacha knows that this side of town isn't the best. Natacha lets down the driver side window halfway so that she can hear the conversation.

"Sorry, buddy." He holds his hands up as to say that he's broke.

"Aww man, you got something. Look at where you and yo lady eatin' at."

"I don't have anything for you, sir." How dare this bum come up to him and demand something?

"Alright, mutha-fucka, I tried to be nice." The bum pulls a gun from under his needlessly long trench coat and gears it towards Felix. Natacha's in the car watching the entire ordeal and pulls her .38 from her purse. Trying quickly to debate whether to interfere or not, she stays cool. Felix wouldn't like her jumping to his defense and she can respect that, but if her presence is needed, she'll gladly oblige.

"Okay, man. No need for all of that." Felix now has his hands in the surrender position. "I'm gonna reach for my wallet." He slowly brings his hands down to his back pocket.

"Hurry up, mutha-fucka."

"Okay." Felix speeds up his slow motion and hands the thief his wallet.

He looks inside and he blazes with anger. "Man there's over three hundred dollars in here. I should shoot yo ass for being stingy as hell." He raises the gun and takes a few steps closer to Felix. "Mutha-fucka!" He shouts and hits Felix on the head with the gun.

Natacha leans over the seats and puts her .38 out the window, letting go two quick, loud shots. The bum falls to his face and she jumps out the car.

"Felix, are you okay?" She kneels down beside him. Natacha is a bit ashamed that one hit on the head took him down like that.

"Yeah, I think so." He says getting to his feet and holding his head. "I thought he had shot me."

"Naw." *'Punk ass,'* she thinks to herself.

"You shot him?"

"I had to, he was gonna kill you."

"When did you start carrying a gun?"

"Felix this isn't the time or place for this. Come on, lets go."

"We have to call the police and wait for them."

"No Felix." She's making her way back to her side of the car. "Come on!"

The couple sits on Natacha's leather sofa and she's holding an ice pack on Felix's head.

"What the hell happened out there, Natacha?" Felix grabs her hand, softly.

"I had to step in. I waited as long as I could."

"But you shot him."

"So you're mad that I shot him?"

"Strangely, no. I'm kind of glad that you did or I'd be dead. But, how... I mean, when...."

SHAN MARIE

"I carry my gun because of people like him. I'm a single woman living alone and I need protection."

"Why didn't you want to call the police?"

"Because my gun isn't registered and it would cause us all kinds of problems."

"I can understand that, I guess. But you're not shaken at all." He looks at her with a suspicious eye.

"I go to the shooting range and practice. I've taken self-defense courses. So I've been prepared for a long time."

"But it doesn't bother you that you killed someone?"

"Not someone like him, no. Not when my life and yours was in danger, no. It wasn't cold-blooded murder. Besides we don't know if he's dead or not."

"He's dead. He looked dead."

"Why don't you go take a shower and unwind a bit." She says it as an order more than a question. "I'll get us a movie to watch."

"Okay."

Felix stays in the shower all of thirty minutes and Natacha knows that he needs every second to calm down. This is one of the reasons why she feels that she can't be with him. Felix knows nothing about the streets. He has all of the book sense and common sense, but no street sense. Natacha feels relieved that he bought her reasoning for not wanting to call the police and hopefully he won't bring it up again.

"I'm glad that we found each other again." Felix runs his hand over her mane.

"Me too."

"It's no accident you know."

"Yeah, I know."

"We're supposed to be together. Listen, Natacha. I know that we have our differences, me being a white-collar brother and you being a gangster woman." He lets out a short laugh; Natacha doesn't think it's funny. "I'm willing to work thru our inconsistencies if you are."

"Maybe it's worth a try." She states, unsure of the decision.

"Since we've already done the dating thing, maybe we should kick it up a notch."

"What do you mean?"

"Being with you tonight, made me realize what I've been missing, outside of your rescuing me. I need you Natacha. I want you baby and I've never stopped loving you."

She has tears in her eyes. "I love you too, Felix."

"Be my wife." He more demands than asks.

"What? Felix that's a hell-of-a notch up."

52

"I know sweetie, but why not? We already know each other. There's no need to go through that phase again. Plus, neither one of us are getting any younger and I want you to bare my children."

"Children? Felix we need to take this one step at a time."

"You don't want to have children?"

"I haven't really thought about it."

"Okay. I guess we can just discuss that later.'

"Yeah."

"We can go and pick up a ring for you sometime this week. We also need to do some furniture shopping for the house."

"Oh yeah, the house."

"What's wrong?"

"I can't live in Kami's old house."

"Why not baby?"

"I just can't."

"There must be a reason." He lifts her chin so that he can see her eyes.

"Listen Felix. There's a lot that you don't know. Trust me we don't need to live there."

"Okay, fill me in on everything that I don't know."

"There are just too many memories there."

"Like what?"

"Like Los!" She shouts out in frustration.

"Los? What about him?"

"He's dead okay. He was murdered and I can't live in his house."

"Wow! I had no idea. How's Kami with all of this?"

"She's handling it."

"Well we'll just have to find another house. I'm sure we can find something just as nice. Probably not for such a great price, but we'll find something."

"If you want me then you'll find something else."

"Okay, done."

"About this marriage thing Felix, I can't say yes right now. Can we just see how things work out?"

"So you want to live together but not be married?"

"We can for a while."

"I don't understand that. Women are always complaining about a man wanting to shack up and never get married. I want to make you my wife and you want to shack up."

"Just for a while. There's no sense in getting married and then divorced a few months later."

"I don't plan on getting a divorce."

"You never know."

"I do know and I want you. This can work, Natacha."

"We'll see, okay."

After a boring love making session, Natacha gives Kamille a call to share the evening's happenings. *"What you doing, shawty?"*

"Sitting here with Jackie smoking."

"You bitches!" They laugh.

"Whatever, you're the one that wanted to go lay up with that lame dude." They laugh again.

"Kami, this shit ain't gon' work."

"What happened?"

"A 'J' tried to rob us tonight."

"What?" Kamille sits up in the lounger, ready to retaliate.

"Hell yeah! We were leaving The Melting Pot and the fool walked up on Felix, pulled out a 'tool' and everything."

"What did you do? Did you have to come to your man's rescue?" Kamille lets out a slight giggle realizing that this is serious but amused at the thought of Felix being held at gun point.

"Hell yeah! I had to pop the dude. He hits Felix on the head and this lame fool goes down like the damn Titanic."

They laugh hard this time. *"Yeah, you need someone with some backbone."*

"I just can't seem to drop this dude though."

"Where is he now?"

"*Sleeping, with his punk ass.*"

"*He's distraught.*" Natacha laughs hysterically and covers her mouth when she realizes that she's being very loud. She doesn't want Felix to hear her making fun of him.

"*Kami, I had to make the fool go lay down and shit. I'm like take a breather, it'll be okay. He wanted me to hold him.*"

"*Hold him?*"

"*Yeah.*"

"*Like you hold a baby?*" Natacha has another outburst of laughter.

"*Bitch, I gotta go before I wake this nigga up.*"

Kamille flips her cell phone closed, laughing at her best friend and her so called man. Jackie is in a daze, so high that she doesn't really know what's going on. "What the hell are you laughing at?" Jackie asks as Kamille rolls another cigar filled with marijuana.

"Natacha's crazy ass."

"What is she doing?"

"Nothing, messing with this square ass dude that can't lay her down right or protect her."

"Oh, she needs to get rid of him."

"That's what I'm saying."

"Y'all have been friends a long time, huh?"

"Since first grade."

"Must be nice to have someone in your life like that."

"Yeah, we should've been sisters."

"You don't talk about your family much. Are you an only child?"

"Yeah, my mom is dead and my dads' in jail." Jackie is silent now. "Why are you so quiet?"

"I just know how it feels to lose someone you love. How long has your mom been dead?"

"Years, I was like seven when she died."

"How'd she die?"

"I don't know. All I know is that she didn't come home one night and my dad said she was dead."

"That's fucked up."

"Yeah it is."

"Girl, what do you have me smoking? This shit got me feeling crazy as hell."

Kamille laughs as Jackie tries to get up from her seat. "That's that good shit, ain't it?"

"Hell yeah, too good. I'm too old for this."

"How old are you Jackie?"

"Forty-seven."

"Same age my mom would be. So how'd you get into the 'game'?"

"I was going to ask you the same thing. I started out selling with my ol' man then we split and I moved to Florida and kept it going."

"I hooked up with Los and he taught me a few things, but I learned the most when he was locked up and I had to do it all by myself."

"You've made quite a name for yourself. I heard about you in Florida and thought, damn this chick is doing her thing in the 'A'."

"I want out."

"Really? Why?"

"I'm tired of it. Folks want to see you dead and fools are not being loyal. I'm tired. I wish Los was here because I don't know what to do."

"Yeah, this life isn't all it's cracked up to be. The messed up thing is that I've been in the 'game' for over twenty years and there's nothing else I know how to do."

"Same here. I was talking to Natacha about getting out of the 'game', but what would I do? Day in and day out; doing what?"

"I don't know."

Kamille finds herself ready to confide in Jackie. "If I had to do it all again I don't know if I'd change anything besides Los being killed. There's something about the power that this life brings. I didn't think that I could be the type of woman that I've become. When I look back as a child I was happy until everyone left me. Then I met Los, my world felt complete again. Now, I'm back to shambles."

"I can tell that you loved him."

"I still do."

"I learned that men can be the worst or best thing to happen to you."

"I think I'm a little naïve when it comes to men."

"Why do you say that?"

"The only man I've ever been with is Los, I don't know any different."

"That has its good and bad points. The good is that you have that longevity in relationships the bad is that you lack experience with men. There are some dudes out there that will smash your heart and leave you with nothing. You just have to be careful. Especially by you being who you are. A lot of men in the 'game' won't be able to handle you being as big and in charge as you are."

"I hope to find someone that can handle me in more ways than one. I would like to fall back and let the men do all the work. I can just chill and take care of home, but then again I don't want to put that much into a man again. I trusted Los with my life, literally and I don't see another man having a hold on me like that again."

"Maybe not but it could still happen."

Bridgett sits up in the bed and throws her legs along the side. As she reaches down to grab her panties, she moans slightly at the pain in her legs. Long nights with the freaky Felix have caused her body to go into daytime convulsions and nighttime spasms.

"Why do you always bring me to this hotel Felix?"

"Don't you like it?" He asks as he slips on his briefs.

"Yeah, but why can't we go to your house or mine?"

"Why would we? We have everything we need right here."

"It's not like you're married or something Felix. We can chill at your house."

"Bridgett, please don't pretend that you don't know what's going on."

"What do you mean by that?"

"I bring you here because of the type of situation that we're in."

"So now I'm a situation?" Bridgett is obviously offended.

"Come on, Bridgett. I'm not the first man that you've done this with."

"Done what?"

"This. The whole reason that we're even here is because that's the type of woman that you are. Why do you think that we come all of the way out here? I'm a businessman and I socialize in very large and important circles. The chance of me running into one of my colleagues out here is slim to none. Why would I take you to my home? That's where I live and my woman sleeps there most nights. There's no way I'd have you in the same bed that she lays her head in."

"What the fuck? Nigga are you serious? So I'm just some hoe you fuck?"

"That's right." Felix finishes getting dressed and grabs his blazer off of the chair.

"So you think Natacha is some good girl or somethin'?"

"She's better than you."

"Fuck you, nigga. Natacha do a lot of dirty shit. I bet you didn't know that she sells dope." Bridgett crosses her legs and gives Felix a 'now what' look.

"What are you talking about?"

"Yeah, nigga. Yo prize ass Natacha slang dope and she don' killed folks so fuck you nigga. Crazy mutha-fucka."

"Calm down. It's not like you didn't know what was going on."

"Fuck you! Yeah, I knew that we were just fuckin' but I didn't know that you was an asshole like this." Felix stands near the door gazing out into space. He thinks back to a few nights ago when Natacha came to his rescue when the guy tried to rob them. He remembers how calm she was and how easily she pulled the trigger. "You hear me talkin' to you?"

"What?" He snaps out of his trance.

"You standin' there thinkin' 'bout that bitch ain't ya?"

"Don't call her that."

"Fuck this shit. Take me home mutha-fucka." Bridgett proceeds to grab her belongings.

"You're lying."

"What?"

Felix takes a few steps towards her. "You're lying. Natacha is nothing like you. There's no way that she lives that type of life."

"Well she does and you right, she ain't shit like me 'cause I wouldn't be caught dead wit' yo lame ass."

"Shut up!" Felix slaps Bridgett's face. "You could never be her. You're just a fuck and that's even getting boring."

"Mutha-fucka." Bridgett charges at him, plunging him into the wall, beating his face and scratching like a wild cat.

Felix grabs her by the hair, pulling her head backwards and punches her full force in the stomach. Bridgett collapses on the floor in tears. "Find your own way home, bitch." He spats and then spits in her face.

"Where in the fuck have you been?" Joe greets Bridgett at the door of her apartment.

"Nowhere."

"Here we go with that shit again. Why you coming home in a cab?"

"I got stuck at a friends' house."

"You think I'm stupid, bitch?"

"No, what are you talking about?" Smack! He slaps her and blood splatters onto the wall beside her. "Wait Joe, please. Okay, I was on a date with this dude." Joe raises his hand again. "Wait. I was checking him out."

"Checking him out for what?"

"I was gonna rob him."

"So where the shit at?"

"He kicked me out before I could do it."

"Bitch!" Smack! "You really think I'm stupid, don't you?" Joes pulls Bridgett by the hair and slaps her a third time.

"Joe please, I was just trying to make you some money." Bridgett tries quickly to get out of a hopeless situation.

"I don't give a fuck. What does that have to do with what I'm talkin' about?"

"I'm about to tell you." She inhales deeply from fear and uncertainty. "He has a lot of money and I know where he lives. We can go rob 'em, you know."

"What kinda money the nigga got?" The dollar bill always catches Joe's attention.

"He got mad money, Joe. The nigga into real estate and be buyin' houses and shit."

"How you know the nigga?"

"Just from around the way."

"What you know about 'em?

"He don't be home some nights and he drive nice ass cars and shit. He's a lame nigga, you know, blue collar type."

"How in the hell you know a blue collar nigga?"

"I told you, just from around the way."

"How the fuck do you know him?" Joe must know everything possible about a 'mark' before he goes in. There's no way he'd bust in someone's crib without knowing anything about them.

"I use to kick it with the nigga, damn."

"Tell me what you know, Bridge."

"I fucked with him a little and the nigga flipped out on me last night over some dumb shit. So now I have a chance to get the nigga back."

"Alright. That's a bet." Bridgett informed Joe of everything that he needed to know. She sits on her bed spilling her guts, through a busted nose and blackened eyes.

7

"**H**EY YOUNG LADY." Kamille is outside her new home planting her garden and an older woman walks up to her holding a pie.

"Hi."

"I'm Mrs. Fletcher from next door. Just wanted to come over and introduce myself." The old woman is definitely from the south.

"Oh, how sweet." Kamille gets up from the ground and brushes her hands off. "It's nice to meet you Mrs. Fletcher, I'm Kami."

"Kami, that's a pretty name for a pretty young woman."

"Thanks."

"I made you a little pie. It's apple. I see you live alone."

"Thank you and yes ma'am I do."

"That's something we didn't do back in my day. A woman let the man get the house but times have surely changed."

"Yeah, these days we gotta do for ourselves. It's hard to find a decent man now a days."

"Yeah, honey I know. I have seven grandsons and ain't but a few of 'em worth anything."

"Yeah."

"Well I won't hold you up, I see you doing your garden and all. But if you need anything or just want to talk I'm right next door."

"Just you and your husband?"

"Oh no, John Henry passed on over to glory a few years back. It's just me, my grandchildren will come over some time, when it's convenient for them, but that's it. You got a lot of land over here."

"Yes ma'am, I always wanted a house with lots of land."

"Nice."

"You want to come in Mrs. Fletcher?"

"Sure baby, I'll sit a spell."

Kamille and Mrs. Fletcher sat and talked for hours about the new house, men and cooking. Mrs. Fletcher taught Kamille how to bake an apple pie and warned her that it's her secret family recipe.

"What's up, Natacha?" Kamille asks opening the front door.

"Shit. Traffic a 'mo-fo' out this way."

"Who you tellin'? That's the only thing I hate about it but I've learned some back roads I'll show you later."

"Good news, 'cause I-75 is satan." They laugh. "Where you get this pie from?"

"My neighbor."

"You know yo' ass is in the country."

"Chick, I'm still in city limits."

"Yeah, but ain't nobody in Decatur gon' give you no damn welcome to the neighborhood pie. The south don' changed and ain't too many nice folks no more."

"Well the old folks don' held on to they southern hospitality."

"Yeah they have. She just brought it over?"

"Yeah, she walked up on me outside. She's sweet as that damn pie too. I never had a grandma and I sho' wouldn't mind letting her stand in."

"Maybe she can teach yo' ass some manners." Natacha flicked a piece of pie at Kamille. "Ronni want to hook up with us tonight."

"What's she been doin'?"
"Shit."

"Where you want to go?"

"I really don't want to go anywhere."

"We can chill at your spot then." Kamille continues as she wraps the pie in foil and sits it on the stove. "What's up with Felix?"

"I don't know. I meant to tell you that I had to tell him that Los was dead 'cause he was talking about living in your old house. He asked questions so I told 'em that Los was murdered. He asked why you didn't mention it when y'all was doing business and I told 'em that it still hurt."

"Cool. You told 'em that he was killed in the house?"

"Naw. He says that he'll just sell the house and find somewhere else to live."

"You're leaving out something, what's up?"

"I don't like having sex with him."

"Too quiet, right?"

"Yeah, that and he's too gentle with the pussy. I need a nigga that can handle me."

"I feel ya. Have you talked to him about it?"

"No."

"Is he small?"

"Naw, he got a nice package and he works it okay, but I need more power in the drill." They laugh.

"Like Ace?"

"Yeah exactly. Don't get me wrong, I can definitely fall head over hills in love with Felix, but you know what I mean."

"Yeah I do. I suggest you talk to him about it."

"I guess I should."

"E is ready for me to get up with his cousin in Detroit."

"So we taking a road trip?"

"Yeah I am, but I guess you should stay and get up with Felix."

"I can do that another time."

"Maybe you should handle it now, Natacha. Don't get the nigga around if you ain't sure about him."

"What about you? You want to ride all the way up there alone with E?"

"I'll be fine. Plus I'm going to ask Tashjma if she wants to go."

Kamille enters Tashjma's room to find her asleep in bed. "Wake up, shawty." She nudges her awake.

"Yeah Kami, what's up?"

"I have to take a ride."

"Where you going?"

"Detroit."

"Business?"

"Yeah."

"Can I stay here?"

"If you want to, but I don't think it's a good idea."

69

"Why not?"

"There's a lot of shit going on right now."

"I'll be okay. I can just do the same thing I did the last time. I won't answer the phone or the door."

"Alright, Natacha will be in town so call her if you need to but stay in the house."

"I will."

"I'll be at Natacha's for a few hours then I'm hitting the road."

"Kami, I need a job." Ronni sits in Natacha's leather recliner, blunt in hand.

"I know we talked about this already." Kamille states aggravated that she even has to speak to this chick after all that she's learned about her lately.

"Put me to work. I can handle a shop."

"Hum." Kamille pulls her blunt and looks over at Natacha. When the ladies have an *All American Smoke Out*, everybody has their own blunt because the only female that Kamille smokes behind is Natacha.

"What you know about running a shop, Ronni?" Natacha asks.

"I know enough, plus I been around you bitches long enough."

"Give me a job too, Kami." Tashjma butts in, high as hell.

"Naw, you don't need to get involved in this shit, we deep enough." Kamille turns her attention back to Ronni. "Why do you keep fucking with your nose?"

"What are you talking about? I need some 'work'. Now, are you gon' put me 'down' or what?" Ronni flicks her nose again, then sniffs.

"You fucking with that shit, Ronni?" Natacha asks.

"What? Hell naw."

"You're showing everything but that junky itch." Kamille states getting up from her seat and heading for Natacha's kitchen. "Come on, Ronni. How do you expect to be over a shop and you putting that shit in yo' nose?"

"I'm not. Where y'all hear this anyway?"

"Spook told Joe and Joe told us. Now, are you gonna be honest or what? I'm telling you right now that I'm not putting you to 'work' until we get this straight." Kamille lays down the law as she comes back to the living room with a glass of Hennessey.

"I did a little bit sometimes." Ronni begins her confession.

"Damn, Ronni!" Natacha is upset that she is the one that put her on'. Kamille was right about Ronni, but she was right about Bridgett.

"But I ain't a junky." Ronni exclaims.

"Then what are you?" Kamille asks.

71

"I'm me."

"Why are you in such a hurry to get some 'work'. You should have plenty of money from the 'snow' you just bought a few weeks ago."

"I sold that and spent the dough already."

"Uh-huh." Natacha doesn't believe a word.

"Natacha, why are you trippin'?" Ronni feels that it's her turn to be upset.

"Because I put you on and now you're screwing up."

"How am I messin' up? What I do on my time is my motherfuckin' business."

"What is rule number one, Ronni?" Natacha takes the leader role and Kamille is very proud of her.

"What rules are you talking about?"

"The fuckin' rules, Ronni. The rules of this game that you're taking so lightly."

"I don't know."

"Don't get high off of your own supply, Ronni. A junky can't be trusted, so you gotta go."

"Go?" Ronnie can't believe that she's being kicked out of the click before she had a chance to really get started.

"Yeah, go." Natacha points toward her front door.

The ladies sit and discuss what just happened with Ronnie in disgust. They determine that it's hard to find good help and people that will stick to the unwritten rules of the game. Natacha's cell rings and she becomes annoyed. "It's Felix again."

"Why don't you want to talk to him?"

"I don't know. He's becoming a nag."

"You want to break it off?"

"I don't know but I guess I should answer his call." Natacha speak with Felix briefly. He demands that she come and see him so that they can talk. She has no idea what he wants to talk about, but she feels obligated to at least hear him out.

Natacha pulls into Felix's driveway to find him waiting for her on the front porch. She takes caution as she walks up the walkway. "Hey, Felix. Why are you outside?"

"Waiting on you." She knew that already.

"Is something wrong?" She stops and stares at him through the screen. She has an uneasy feeling but isn't sure whether to be afraid or not.

"Just come in, Natacha." She does and takes a seat next to him in one of the loungers.

The tension can be cut with a knife as they sit in silence. All that's heard in the crickets and critters making their nightly noises. "So what is it Felix."

"Can we just be in each others presence for a few minutes?"

"Of course we can." The silence is deafening. Felix reaches over and grabs Natacha's hand. He holds it tight while starring off into space. A few minutes pass and Natacha can't take it any longer. "Felix, what's wrong?"

"I love you, Natacha."

"I know, Felix."

"Are you going to marry me?"

"I don't know if I'm ready for that."

"What does Kamille do for a living?"

"She dabbles in a lot of things. Why do you ask?"

"What do you do?"

"Felix, why all the questions?"

"Just answer me, Natacha. What do you do?"

"I don't have a job, Felix. You know that."

"How do you live?"

"I have inheritance from my grandparents." Natacha comes up with that lie very fast.

"The night the guy tried to rob us..." He pauses.

"Yes, what about it?"

"You weren't shaken at all when you shot him."

"I was a little upset about it, Felix. It's not that big of a deal because he was a creep. He tried to rob you and that makes him a crook and thief."

"Why do you carry a gun?"

"For protection against looser like him. I told you this already." Natacha is getting more and more upset as Felix goes on with his questions. She takes her hand from his grip and stands up. "What is this, Felix? What is it that you really want to ask me?"

"Why are you so defensive?"

"I don't like to be questioned. Especially like this."

"Are you doing anything illegal?"

"No, where are you getting this from?"

"I'm just putting two and two together. You carry a gun, you kill a man and leave him there. You just kill him and that's it. I cried, you didn't."

"So this is all because I'm not a punk?"

"I'm no punk either, Natacha." Felix stands while saying this. He can't allow his manhood to be threatened.

"You sure acted like one when you got hit on the head with a pistol."

"I'm not around things like that, Natacha. That was the first time I'd ever been in a situation like that."

"It's okay that you were scared."

"I wasn't scared."

"Yes you were and it's okay. I'm from the hood, Felix. Things like that happen all the time where I'm from."

"So you're use to it?"

"Exactly."

"I just wonder how you can take things so lightly."

"What can I say? It's a gift."

"Sit back down, Natacha."

"I don't want to. I think I should leave."

"No, you can't leave."

"You don't tell me what to do."

"I don't want you to leave, Natacha." Tears begin to flow down his face.

"Why are you crying?"

"I just love you so much and I need you."

"Felix this is getting too heavy for me right now." Natacha wants to tell him how much of a weak punk he is but decides against it.

"I want you to stop hanging around Kamille."

"What? Why?"

"I have a feeling that her husband was a bad guy and she's probably mixed up in his mess too. You don't need to be around that."

"Kami and I have been friends since we were kids. There's no way I'm going to cut her off."

"She's more important than me? Than us?"

"Yes she is Felix. She is more than a sister could ever have been to me. You have no idea what we've been through together."

"You'd let me go before her?"

"Yes, without a second thought."

"That's really messed up, Natacha. Her I am trying to make a life for us and you're putting friends before me like we're kids."

"Look at it how you want to. I don't even know if I can spend the rest of my life with you and you want me to make a life changing decision like that. What do you expect me to do?"

"You don't know if you can spend the rest of your life with me?"

"No, I don't."

"Why not?"

"There are several things Felix and I don't want to get into them now."

"I need to know what you're talking about."

She doesn't want to hurt his feelings. "There are things that I don't know if I can get pass, that's all."

"What things?"

Natacha sits and Felix follows suit. "The sex for one."

"You don't like the way I make love to you?"

"Not all the time. You have good motion but things are so bland. No excitement or thrills."

"We can fix that.'

77

"Okay, then there is stuff like when the junky tried to rob you. I had to protect you and it should've been the other way around."

"What was I to do with a gun at my head?"

"That's just it, Felix. I'm use to being with men that carry guns and I don't have to be afraid around them."

"So you want me to be a hoodlum?"

"Sometimes I wish you were a little rougher around the edges."

"I see. A blue collar man is too boring for you."

"I love that you're educated and well spoken and even when you correct my grammar I know you're doing it because you care. But yes, I get bored Felix."

"Okay, so in order for us to be together I need to get a gun, take some fucking 'how to be a thug' classes and fuck you instead of making love to you."

"That's not necessary, Felix."

"No, no, let me get this straight. I'm a good man, living a legal, drug free life and that's not good enough for you. You want me to do jail time, send you pen pal letters and have conjugal visits while my baby mama is calling playing on your phone."

She can't stand the sarcasm. "Whatever Felix, I'm out of here."

"Should I slap you around a little bit too?" He yells as she goes down the walkway back to her Jeep. "A few punches to the face every now and then."

"Fuck you, Felix." She flips him off as she gets in to the Jeep.

"We can fight every night so the police can come lock me up. Then you can post bail the next morning and we do it all over again."

8

"IT'S BLACK AS HELL UP HERE."

Kamille is enjoying her view of the Motor City, Detroit, as she gawks at the African American strangers. She feels a little uncomfortable without Natacha but she wants her to handle her business.

"Yeah, things a definitely not the same though." Ethan has his eyes on everything but the city. He's used to seeing these streets and has better intentions for the trip.

"Hell naw!" Kamille stares out in disbelief.

"What?"

"Is that really a black fist?"

"Yep."

"I thought folks were bullshitting when they talked about the black fist of Detroit."

"Naw, it's for real."

"So what do you mean things aren't the same?"

"Everything is closing down. All the plants and warehouses, folks don't have no jobs up here."

"So business is probably pretty good then?" They laugh at the fact that dope sells go sky high when people are out of work. Even though it's not really funny, it works out well for those in the 'game'.

"Hell yeah, my folks is full as hell up here." Ethan looks over at Kamille sitting in the passenger seat of his Navigator, laughing. He admires how her smile lights up wherever she is and how soft she really is, even though she has to play hard. "What's up wit' you, Kami?"

"What do you mean?" She manages to ask in between laughing and catching her breath.

"You seeing somebody?"

Kamille becomes extremely serious as her postures turns to an upright position. She crosses her legs and looks over at Ethan who is watching her every move. "Why do you ask?"

He stares at her intensely, noticing everything that has suddenly changed about her. "I was hoping that we could chill after we handle business."

"Actually, I am seeing someone. Nothing too serious but it could become something."

"Are you happy?"

"Content."

"Can we chill then?"

"What do you have in mind, Ethan?" She cuts her eyes at him.

"Why did you ask like that?" He smiles an oleaginous smile that leaves Kamille wanting to know more about this slim thug from College Park. All is on her mind, though, is killing him. Maybe he didn't have anything to do with her mother's murder but his father did.

"You want to fuck me?"

"Damn girl!"

"Well? Do you?"

"Yeah I do."

"No thanks."

"Why not?"

"I'm getting fucked pretty well right now, so I'm good." She lies through her beautiful white teeth. Kamille yearns for a man's touch, especially her own man. She knows that will never happen again. Replacing Carlos is not an option. No man can make her feel the way that he did. She has to just move on and live her life, but it's hard as hell to allow another man to touch her in the ways that she's used to.

"Damn."

"Is your father still living?" Straight to the point.

82

"Yeah, why?"

"His name is Red, right?"

"Yeah, why?"

"He still in the game?"

"What's up, Kami? Why so many questions about my dad?"

"Just wondering."

"No, he got out the game years ago. He owns a mortuary now."

"So why don't you join the family business?"

"Shit, I belong to the streets, shawty."

"I feel ya. So did you run the streets with your dad when you were little?"

"Sometimes. For the most part he tried to keep me out of it, except for when he was drunk."

"So he had a drinking problem?" She pretends to make small talk.

"Yeah, he'd get drunk as hell and then drag me around with him to collect his money."

"He sold a lot of dope?"

"Yeah him and Scotty started out together."

"Is that right?" Kamille knows this already but has to act surprised.

"Yep. They were running shit for real back then."

Back in Atlanta, Ronni is attempting to kick her habit and prove to Kamille and Natacha that she can run her own shop.

"Naw, Spook. I don't want any."

"You sure, girl? This some good shit." Spook says while flicking his nose and starring at Ronni's breasts.

"Yeah, I'm sure. As a matter-of-fact, I have to go." She gets up from his fake leather sofa.

"Hold up, shawty." Spook grabs her arms and pulls her back down beside him. "Why you in a hurry to leave?" Ronni has noticed that he's gotten bolder since Kamille promoted him to two shops.

"I got some stuff I gotta do, that's all."

"Naw, I think you running."

"Running from what?"

"You scared."

"Scared of what nigga?"

"Scared of this dope dick."

"You know I ain't scared. I just have something to do."

"You can't put it off?"

"Naw."

"What you gotta do?"

"Damn nigga, can I do me, please?" Ronni rummages her brain for an excuse. Truth is, she's breaking under the pressure and needs to get away.

"Fo' sho', but take a run with me first."

"Where?"

"Just come on. I got a job and there's a lot of dough in it for you."

Meanwhile in Detroit, Kamille and Ethan are getting to know each other a little better while they wait on his cousins to show up at the spot.

"So you meant what you said Kami? We can't spend some time together?"

"Yeah I meant it. It's a conflict of interest." Kamille sits in a shack of a house in the heart of the ghetto. She's compulsively afraid that one of God critters will find there way to her soft skin.

"What conflict?"

"You and Los didn't get along. How could I get with a dude that hated my ol' man?" *'Never mind that fact that your father killed my mother mutha-fucka.'* Kamille thinks to herself

"I didn't hate the nigga. Just didn't agree with some of his tactics, that's all."

"Whatever your reasons were, I can't fuck with you on that level." The front door opens and appears to be on the verge of collapsing. A butch looking female enters with a young looking boy following her.

"What up, E?" The female speaks first. Ethan gets up from his seat to greet his family.

"What it do pimp?" They continue with a short hand shake. "This is Kami." Ethan gestures in Kamille's direction.

"What's up?" She gives a 'what's up' node as she releases herself from her seat. "You are?" She asks extended her hand to the dike first.

"Tommie."

"And you?" She asks the younger cousin.

"Denarus."

"Okay cool. Can we get to business?"

"Yeah." The boy speaks. "E said that you got the fire shit."

"True."

"Yeah we need to get the 'frig' full you know."

"I can help with that. How much you want to spend?"

"I got enough to shop big." Denarus walks over to an old imitation painting on the wall. Kamille secretly laughs at the familiar art of the dogs playing poker. He pulls the painting down and proceeds to open a hidden safe. 'Not too dumb for a young cat', Kamille thinks to her self. Denarus pulls out several rubber banded wads of cash. "Each one of these is five-thousand." He places a few on the dining room table.

"E says that you need a few pounds of green and some weight."

"Yeah, that's good."

Kamille sells to the two and makes sure that they have a contact number for her. "You know some more folks that need 'work' let me know; my shop's always open."

Ronni and Spook ride west of Atlanta to Austell in his Impala.
"Where are we going, Spook?"
"Joe asked me to handle this lil' nigga up here."
"How much do I get?"
"We gotta see what the hell he got first."
"What do you know about him?"
"You got a lot of questions."
"I'm supposed to. I don't know what's going on." Ronni is a little reluctant to do a 'job' with Spook. He has a bad reputation of fucking up shit like this. However, she needs to get some stripes to help prove to Kamille that she can handle herself. *'If Joe knows then Kami knows'*, she thinks and convinces herself that this will be for her good.
"Yeah, but chill out. I swear you need to hit this shit and mellow the fuck out." Spook holds up a pipe filled with crack for Ronni to enjoy.
"No thanks, Spook."
"Come on shawty, damn."
Giving into temptation, Ronni grabs the pipe from Spook and lights it. Her head thrust

backwards as the drug begins to take effect. "Damn."

"I tried to tell you shawty. This shit is off the chain. Kami got that good shit, shawty I swear." Another hit and Ronni is spaced out and having trouble getting her eyes to focus.

They pull across the street from a house that must be worth all of a million dollars. Ronni can't believe her eyes. The biggest house that she'd ever been inside was Kamille's old spot and this house seems to be even larger. They watch as a man gets out of a silver BMW and enters the house.

"That's that fool." Spook speaks as he peers at the man from across the street.

"We gon' do this in broad day light?"

"Hell yeah."

"Why can't we wait for a few hours, let the sun go down?"

"Girl, come on." Spook opens the driver side door and hops out.

Ronni on the other hand gets out of the Impala with ease. She's so high that focus is a far off attainment. The duo walks across the street, Spook handing Ronni a 'tool' along the way.

Spook knocks on the man's door and stands beside Ronni out of sight. "Now, when he come to the door just say that your car broke down or something. Just get him to open the door."

"Okay." Ronni states not fully understanding the plan.

"Who is it?" The voice comes from behind the door.

"Sir, can you help me?"

"What do you need?" The man looks from behind a curtain on the side window.

"My car... It's broke." Ronni feels a sudden rush and begins to bounce up and down.

"What?"

"My car stopped and I need to use a phone. Do you have one please?"

"Yeah, hold on." The man disappears from the small window.

"Stop all that damn moving, Ronni." Spook orders from beside her.

"I can't help it. I could jump off a damn cliff right now."

The front door creaks and the two stop their conversation. "Here you go." The man opens the door and hands Ronni a cordless phone.

"Step back mutha-fucka." Spook steps to the front almost knocking Ronni to the ground. Then she noticed that they weren't wearing any masks. The only time you do dirt without a mask is if you're not planning on leaving any witnesses.

"What in the hell is this?" The man states as he backs up with his hands in the air.

"It's a Jack move nigga, now get yo' ass in the house." The man does as he's told and Spook follows right behind him. "Yo'." He calls to Ronni who is still standing in the open door.

"Yeah."

"Come in and close the fucking door shawty, damn." She does as told and the orders begin rolling in. "Get some rope or something to tie his ass up with."

"Look man, there's no need for all of that." The man speaks in fear and confusion. "I got money in the house, you can have it all, just don't kill me."

"I'll think about it, nigga." Spook likes being in charge. He flicks his nose and waits for Ronni to return. "Girl, where the hell you at?"

Ronni runs from an elevated living area. "All I found was some cords."

"Whatever, just tie his hands and legs." He faces the man and hits him on the head with the butt of the gun. "Get on yo' knees."

"Okay, whatever you say." The man flops to his knees with his arms still raised in surrender. Ronni ties his hands and feet as tight as she can and waits for the next order.

"Where's the money, nigga?" He asks as the barrel of the gun touches the man's right temple.

"There's a safe in my bedroom, in the closet; upstairs, third door on the left. The combination is 18-46-7."

"Stay here and watch this nigga, I'll be back." Ronni pulls out her gun and points it towards the man.

Upstairs Spook gets into the safe and cleans it out. He thinks it's about twenty thousand in there. Then he moves to the dresser and sees all kinds of goodies; two Rolex watches, gold bracelets and cufflinks. He finds a trash can in the bathroom and pours the trash on the floor. He dumps the jewelry and money in the bag and looks for more valuables.

Back downstairs, Ronni continues to bounce and pace the floor with anxiousness.

"Why are you doing this?" The man asks Ronni.

"I don't know mister, will you just please be quiet."

"But I don't know you people. Have I hurt you in any way?"

"You must've fucked with someone."

"No, I haven't. Why are you doing this?"

91

"I said I don't know. nNow shut the fuck up." Ronni is getting restless and needs to get some air.

"Alright nigga I got what I came for." Spook comes back from his house hunt.

"Good. Are you going to leave now?" The man asks looking up at Spook with tears in his eyes.

"Yeah, we out." The man lowers his head in relief. Spook looks at Ronni and gives a nod. She's unsure what he wants her to do. He stares at her with his brows raised.

"What?" She whispers.

"Do it, got-damn it."

The man looks up in fear. He turns to see Ronni. "Please lady, don't." He cries.

Spook is nervous enough without Ronni freezing up. "Got-damn it, Ronni. Kill this mutha-fucka." He yells.

"No! Please don't." The man begins to attempt a crawl. He tries to get away from the intruders as fast as he can, but he can't.

"He won't be still." Ronni screams out in disorientation.

"Kill him!" Spook yells again.

Ronni swiftly walks over to the man and point the gun at him.

"Lady, I'll give you anything. Please don't!" He continues to cry out for pity.

Ronni shakes as she ponders what to do.

"Finish this shit so we can go, Ronni."

"Please, please, please." He cries more. Ronni looks down at the man's tear drenched face and whispers, "I'm sorry" and pulls the trigger.

"You need a man like me, Kami. A real nigga."

Kamille looks over at Ethan as they ride back to Georgia. "I'm good, E."

"Give me a chance. Shit, I always thought you was fine as hell. When we get back to the 'A' we can go chill at my spot. You know I live in them expensive ass penthouses downtown. My shit is on the top floor, we can have a nice dinner on the roof or something. "

"Thanks, but no thanks."

"Come on, shawty."

"Nigga, back the fuck off me."

"Damn, yo fucking mouth gon' get you hurt."

"By who, mutha-fucka?"

"Look, I was just trying to holla."

"I don't want to get down with you like that E, damn. What do you want me to say? I ain't fucking with you like that." Just then Kamille's cell phone rings. *"Hey."* She sees that it's Natacha.

"What's good?"

"*Not a damn thing.*"

"*What's wrong?*"

"*Later.*"

"*You on your way back?*"

"*Yeah.*"

"*Alright. I stopped by the house to check on Tashjma but she's not there.*"

"*I told that lil' girl to stay her ass in the house. You got shit straight with Felix?*"

"*Naw, I ain't heard from his ass today.*"

"*Alright, well I'll be there in a few hours.*"

"*Cool.*"

9

KAMILLE, JACKIE, AND NATACHA
**TAKE A RIDE THROUGH ATLANTA.
COLLEGE PARK, EAST POINT, AND WEST
DECATUR TO CHECK ON THE SHOPS.** This
is the last day for them running College Park and
East Point, for the time being, so they're basically
riding through to say some fake good-byes and see
if anyone's heard from Tashjma.

"What's up, Traz?" Kamille enters his shop
on a mission for information.

"Hey, Kami. What's good?"

"I'm looking for Tashjma. You seen her?"

"Naw, but I'll get the word out."

"Do that."

**The ladies ride down Cleveland Avenue
just to check on things.** Kamille sees some

unfamiliar young guys standing in her territory selling weed.

"Who are those niggas?" Kamille asks knowing that Natacha doesn't know the answer.

"I don't know but they pushing weed on that corner."

"I see." Kamille parks her SUV on the corner and the ladies hop out. "Ay, youngstas, what's up?"

"Shit, you ladies want some 'green'?" One of the young thugs in training asks.

"Naw." Kamille response.

"Ay, I know you. You Los girl." Another youngsta states.

"Yeah."

"I hear you the one running shit. I hear you ain't to be fucked wit' either."

"You hear right." Kamille assures. "That's what I want to holla at y'all about. Can we take a walk?"

"Fo' sho'." There's only three of the young thugs and they all follow Kamille and Natacha down the block. They stop to chat right in front of some woods behind a gas station.

"So y'all know this is my spot y'all settin' up shop at?"

"We do now." The same youngsta' speaks with a serious expression on his face.

"So this is how it works. You can have this block, but you shop with me. If you can't do that, you move."

"What if we don't?" This skinny, wide-eyed nigga is asking some dumb ass questions. Shit he should already know the answer to. The ladies can tell that he ain't got shit and probably never will. He look like he smoking rocks and he holds his dick entirely too much.

"I'm sure you can answer that question."

"Fuck that, we been on this corner for a minute and shit is good. I ain't movin'." He continues.

"That's cool. It just means that we do business."

"I'm cool with that. That means that we part of yo' shit right?" Kamille likes this nigga. He's the one that's doin' the most talkin' and the one who recognized her.

"You start at the minimum. Y'all ain't slangin' shit but weed. I got enough of that on my team. I wouldn't mind puttin' you down with some real work though."

"Shit, that sounds good to me."

"What's your name?"

"Donta'."

"Alright and what about you?" Kamille points to the quiet dude.

"Rashad." He's a small kid, can't be but a hundred pounds soaking wet.

"And you?" Kamille asks the angry nigga.

"Man, I ain't answering to a bitch." Jackie walks up on the little scrub and puts her .38 to his head, looks at him in the eyes and pulls the trigger.

"Did you have to use that loud ass .38?" Kamille asks.

"I didn't like the nigga. He would've caused too much shit with his fuckin' mouth. Ay, help me put 'em in these woods." Jackie is speaking to Rashad and he does as asked.

"That was yo' folk, Donta'?" Kamille asks the nigga 'cause he looks scared and has teared the fuck up.

"Naw, I mean yeah, but I didn't know him like that." She can tell that he's lying, they probably were best friends, but he knows to chill. Smart!

"That nigga owed me twenty bucks though." Rashad states with a regretful look plastered on his face. He wishes like hell that he'd got his change before all of this.

"Check his pockets. He probably got it on him." Rashad pushes back through the thick brush, searches the corpse and pulls out almost two ounces of weed and ninety dollars.

"Welcome to the family." Kamille smiles as if a dead body wasn't just put in some woods and covered with leaves. "I'll met y'all here at one o'clock tomorrow, don't be late."

"Kami, you okay?" Natacha asks her best friend knowing that she's worried about her adopted child.

"Yeah, but where in the fuck could she be?"

"I don't know."

Jackie feels Kamille's pain and wants to do what she can to help. "Where does she hang out?"

"Shit, that's what I need to know. All I know is that she's friends with this little bitch that I don't like named Dallas."

"Why don't you like her?" Jackie asks.

"The bitch just rubs me the wrong way."

"What are we going to do to find her?"

"I don't know, I guess I need to get in the streets." Just then there's a knock at the door. Kamille jumps up from her seat and rushes to the front door. She snatches it open and sees Sylvester standing there with a huge grin on his face. She stares at him with curiosity.

"Ain't you gon' invite me in?"

"Yeah, come in." She steps back to clear the doorway.

"What's up, why do you look so freaked out?"

"A friend of mine is missing."

"Well, I'll let you handle yo' business, just show me to my room." Sylvester stops in his tracks, starring across the room. He seems to have lost all breathing abilities and looks as if he's about to faint. Kamille follows his eyes to Jackie. "What the fuck? Victoria?" Kamille and Natacha stare at one another is confusion.

"Excuse me?" Jackie is dumbfounded.

"Excuse me, hell! You're supposed to be dead."

"Sly what in the fuck are you talking about?" Kamille can't take the suspense any longer.

"That's yo' fuckin' mama. That's what I'm talkin' about." Kamille stares at Jackie and sees for the first time, herself. She can't breathe and her heart seems to be pounding at ten thousand beats per second.

"Jackie, what is he talking about?" Natacha asks. She's becoming upset because if Jackie is Kamille's mother shit is about to get real ugly, real fast.

"I don't know, Natacha."

Sylvester lets out a loud, annoying sigh. "Natacha, her name ain't no fuckin' Jackie. What? You think you can have surgery on yo' face and I wouldn't know who you are? I fucked you for twenty years *Victoria.*" Sylvester tosses his bags on the floor.

"Fuck you!" Jackie's confusion turns to pure anger.

"Naw, fuck you!"

"Wait a got-damn minute!" Kamille yells at the top of lungs. She reaches behind her back and pulls her .45 out and aims for Jackie's head. "You better talk and I mean quick."

"Alright Kami, calm down." Jackie stands afraid with her hands raised in surrender.

"Don't tell me to fucking calm down!" She's still screaming and her face has turned a beat red. "What in the fuck is he talking about?"

"I didn't know this mutha-fucka was getting out of jail." Jackie states frantically.

"Is it true?"

Sylvester butts in, "hell yeah, it's true."

Kamille points her gun towards Sylvester, "shut the fuck up, Sly." Aiming back at Jackie she asks, "Is it true?"

"I was going to tell you, Kami."

"Bitch!" Bang! Bang! Jackie and Sylvester hit the floor in fear of the gun shots hitting one of them. "All these fucking years and you've been in fucking Florida?"

"Kami, calm down." Natacha approaches her friend with caution.

"You're going to kill me?" Jackie asks.

"If I wanted to kill you, you'd be dead already."

"Hold on Kami, I'm no punk either so maybe we should just take a minute to talk about this."

"Talk about what?" Kamille allows Natacha to take her .45 out of her grip. "Let's start with your death Jackie or Victoria or whatever the fuck your name is. How about we talk about all the fucking years I had to live without a mother. Maybe we can start with you leaving me with this mutha-fucka." Kamille points to Sylvester.

"Wait a second, Kami..." Sylvester attempts to defend himself.

"Shut the fuck up, Sly! You left me and let your punk ass brother fuck with me when ever he felt like it, so you shut the fuck up."

"What?" Jackie knows nothing about Kamille being molested in her childhood. "What did Lester do to you?"

"Don't look worried now. I tell you what, both of you lying mutha-fuckas get the fuck out of my house."

"Kami, I don't have anywhere to go." Sylvester is telling the truth. There's no where for him to lay his head or get food to eat.

"I wouldn't give a fuck. I'm not giving you another chance to leave me. Get out!"

The next day Kamille meets the new thugs to teach them a few things about the 'game'. She's gotten them both enough guns to hold down an entire city. Whether or not they know how to use them, she'd just have to wait and find out.

After last night Kamille is not really in the mood for this but business must go on and she still hasn't found Tashjma.

"So Rashad what part of town do you live in?" Kamille asks just wanting to get to know the boys a little better.

"West Atlanta." They're at one of the shops in a back room separating dope.

"Born and raised?"

"Yep, I'm a Grady baby."

"Here, weigh that." Kamille tosses a bag of cocaine to Rashad. "What about you Donta'?"

"Same."

"Y'all might know my little sister."

"What's her name?" Donta' asks.

"Tashjma."

"I know a Tashjma but she's a hoe."

"Oh yeah."

"Yep."

"What about Dallas?"

"I know freaky ass Dallas. She used to fuck wit' my homeboy Fruit. He got killed though." Rashad speaks with a look of disgust on his face.

"She's crazy as hell too." Kamille is sure that they're talking about the right Dallas now. She thinks back to the three dudes that tried to kill Tashjma and sees Fruit pleading for his life.

"Yeah." Donta' interjects. "They say she always been crazy."

"Oh yeah, why's that?"

"Something about her sister getting killed when she was little." Donta' continues.

"What happened?"

"I don't know the whole story but some chick pushed her in front of a train or some shit."

Kamille stops bagging the drugs and listens with more interest. "When was this?"

"Years ago." Rashad states as he opens a large pack of weed bags. "Dallas was a little girl."

"What train station was it?"

"I don't know."

Donta' seems to remember more. "Kensington I think." Kamille's heart drops. Dallas is the little girl who was at the train station when she killed that girl Stephanie. She thinks and wonders if Dallas knows that it was her that pushed her sister in front of that train.

"Y'all know where Dallas hangs out?"

Kamille calls Natacha and has her meet them at the spot Dallas is known to be at. They sit in her SUV parked in some abandoned apartments. Rashad and Donta' get out seeing if anyone is occupying the apartment.

"Remember that girl Stephanie?" Kamille asks Natacha.

"Naw, from where?"

"Remember when we were in school and that chick kept saying that she was fucking Los and all that shit? The one that always wanted to fight me?"

"Yeah, now I do. She was ugly with that huge gap between her teeth."

"Yep."

"What about her?"

"That's Dallas' sister."

"Dallas who? That girl Tashjma be with?"

"Yeah."

"So what?"

"You don't think that's odd?"

"Coincidental, but not odd. Stephanie got killed years ago didn't she?"

"Yeah."

"How'd she die?"

"She got hit by a train."

"Damn, that's nasty."

"I killed her." Kamille is relieved to have come clean about her first murder. Even though it was self defense, the entire experience still haunts her.

"What?" Natacha looks over at her friend; confused.

"I threw her in front of that train."

"What in the fuck? When? Why? What happened?"

"We started fighting at the train station. I was sick of that bitch talking shit about fucking Los. The train was coming and I took the opportunity. She had a little girl with her."

"Dallas?"

"I think so."

"Why didn't you ever tell me about this?"

"No one knew but that little girl. I was scared that I was going to jail. I never even told Los."

"So what are you thinking, Kami?"

"I think that girl Dallas knows that I killed her sister. Everything about the little bitch is just off. I never liked her ass."

Donta' and Rashad come back to the car to give their bad news. "We don't see nobody."

"Alright, get in."

The boys say that they don't know where Dallas lives so Kamille rides to the burger place she works at. Kamille goes in to ask questions. "Excuse me, sir." She addresses the man in the manager's uniform.

"Yes ma'am, can I help you?"

"Is Dallas here?"

"No, I haven't seen Dallas in a few weeks, she quit. Is there something that I can do for you?"

"Actually, I need to ask you a few questions if I can."

The man looks at her with suspicion. "And you are?"

"Her aunt."

"Oh."

"May we go into your office?"

"Sure." The man gestures to the door marked 'employees only'.

The manager's office is small, dirty and smells like stale fast food. The walls are spotted with all kinds of smut and markings. There are papers and folders everywhere.

"A little disorganized?" Kamille can't help but to make a comment.

"A little."

She looks at his name tag. "Listen Walter, I haven't seen my niece in a few years. Her mother called me crying saying that she doesn't know where she is. I just need a little help."

"I don't know what I can do for you Ms…"

"Gordon."

"Ms. Gordon I haven't heard anything from Dallas. She didn't even come to pick up her last check.

"Could you just tell me what address she put in her application? Just to be sure that she didn't put anything different from her home address."

"I can't do that Ms. Gordon."

"Sure you can." Kamille pulls a wad of cash from her jacket pocket. She grabbed a few thousand from her stash in the SUV; for bribery purposes.

"Your offer is very tempting Ms. Gordon, but I can't help you." Walter diverts his eyes away from the money before him.

"What do you make here Walter, twenty-five thousand a year? I'm sure that you can use a little extra cash. Just do me this one favor, please for my niece."

"I don't know, Ms. Gordon."

Kamille pulls out a second roll of cash, this one twice the size as the one before. She slides them both across the junky manager's desk. "Please."

"Get anything?" Natacha asks back in the car.

"Yeah, I got the address she put on her application." They ride to the address given by Walter and end at a shack in west Atlanta. Junkies and bums are hanging around; Kamille pulls in front of the house and the group gets out.

Rashad knocks on the door and they watch as the torn screen door bounces up against the frame of the house. He knocks again; still no answer.

"What are we gonna do now, Kami?" Donta' asks.

"Let's check the back." They walk through the unkempt landscaping, jumping the short fencing surrounding the yard. Kamille walks up a few stairs to the back door and knocks. No answer. "Fuck it." She kicks the door open.

They enter the dark, smelly home to find it damn near abandoned. There's a half eaten bologna sandwich on the kitchen table with roaches finishing the meal. The group splits and walks around the house in search of anything that can lead them to Tashjma.

"Come look at this, Kami." Natacha calls from one of the back rooms.

"What is it?"

Natacha holds up a picture of Stephanie, the exact way that Kamille remembers her. She gets chills looking at the ghost in the photos so she turns away.

"Nigga. wake up!" Kamille yells at one her newest protégés. Donta' sits in the back of the SUV head back, mouth open and snoring like he's never slept before.

"Huh." He answers his new boss.

Natacha is agitated. "We on a stake-out nigga, wake up."

"How long we gon' be here?" He asks through his sleeping eyes.

"She gotta come here and when she does we will be waiting." Kamille answers. It's already midnight and they've been there for hours.

"Why you think she got yo' sister?" Rashad speaks to assure Kamille of his consciousness.

"I just know she does."

"When she get here are we gonna kill her?"

"After we find Tashjma, *y'all* are going to kill her."

Natacha smiles at her best friend's authority. The boys are silent, thinking about the activities that will take place soon. They didn't have any personal vendetta against Dallas but it doesn't matter and they know that. Now that they're apart of Kamille's family, they do as they are told. Besides, they have to earn some props with Kamille and taking out some young whore is an easy enough job.

Rashad sees a shadow from afar coming down a hill near the back of one of the apartment buildings. "What's that?"

Everyone looks in the direction that Rashad is starring. "I can't be sure that it's her but it's definitely a female." Natacha stares intensely at the figure in the night. They watch as she disappears behind one of the abandoned buildings.

"Let's go." Kamille opens her door and jumps out.

The group walks with fast paces with Kamille leading the bunch. They make a lot of noise walking through piles of leave, making crackling sounds along the way. They reach the rear of the same building that the shadow disappeared behind. Kamille peeks around into the walk way and is met with the barrel of a 9mm pistol. "I've been waiting on you, Kami." The voice is familiar. Kamille stares as the shadow comes into full view. Dallas stands scared, afraid who she's approaching. Afraid of the outcome of this situation. "Walk forward."

Kamille does as she's told. Natacha knows not to make herself noticed. There's no sense in all of them being held at gun point by this little girl. She knows exactly how Kamille would handle it, so she motions for the boys to stay back.

Dallas walks Kamille into one of the vacant apartments. She sees Tashjma lying on the floor sleep, unconscious, dead, she doesn't know. Dallas closes the door and motions for Kamille to sit on the floor. "Sit down." She orders since Kamille ignored her gesture.

"I'm good."

"Sit down." She yells but Kamille can hear and see the fear that she's holding.

"What's up. Dallas? What's wrong with Tashjma?

"She's just high off some good shit, that's all. Now, sit down before I blow your brains out."

"You're not going to shoot me, Dallas."

"How do you figure that?"

"You're shaking. You've never even pulled a trigger before."

"You're right, I am scared. Maybe I should push you in front of a train instead."

Kamille is pissed that this little bitch has her at a stand still. She has faith that her crew will back her up shortly though. "Look got-damn it, put the fucking gun down and I might not chop yo' lil' ass up."

POW! Dallas shoots one shot towards the ceiling and Kamille flinches a little. Doing so pisses her off even more. "You killed my sister, bitch. I'm gonna chop you the fuck up."

"Yeah right, bitch. You don't have the balls to do it. You've gone too far already, Dallas. Why'd you have to fuck with Tashjma, huh? What the fuck has she done to you? If you want me then get me."

"She ain't done shit to me. But you have and I'm gonna hurt you like you hurt me." Dallas approaches Tashjma's still body and aims at her head.

"Stephanie should've stopped fucking with me. I tried to get her to calm down. She made me do it."

"Shut up, bitch." She aims the gun back at Kamille which is what Kamille wants her to do. As long as she stays away from Tashjma everything is fine.

"She kept on until I had to push her in front of that train."

"Shut up!"

"I should've pushed you too. But I spared you because you were so young."

"Fuck you!" Dallas pulls the trigger again almost shooting Kamille, but she ducks and pulls her .45 from her back. With the gun squared on Dallas' head Kamille stares at her with guilt. Tashjma is lying there doped up because of her. She should've seen this coming.

"I'm really sorry about your sister Dallas, I am. But..." POW! A single shot rings out and Dallas hits the floor. Rashad stands in the hall with his 'tool' smoking.

10

KAMILLE GOES INTO TASHJMA'S
ROOM WITH A BOWL OF CHICKEN SOUP.
"Here you go, Tashjma."

"I'm not hungry, Kami."

"You need to eat; come on and sit up."

"I can't shake this feeling of being tired."

"It's the drugs she gave you. It'll wear off
after while."

Tashjma sits up in her bed looking like
she's been hit by a truck. "I can't believe she went
to that extreme."

"Yeah, her head was fucked up. I wasn't
going to kill her, Tashjma. I wanted to try and
talk her down but Rashad killed her before I could
do that."

"I'm glad she's dead. That bitch was crazy.
I should've listened to you when you wanted to get
rid of her earlier."

"It's okay, we live and we learn." The door bell rings and Kamille excuses herself. "Who is it?"

"Kami, its Victoria." Kamille pauses for a moment and tries to calm down. It's been a while since she last saw her mother and she's not sure that she's able to handle another encounter. "Can we talk, Kami?"

Kamille opens the door unsure of what's about to happen. "What do you want?"

"Can I come in?"

"I don't allow strangers in my home. I'll come outside." The mother and daughter duo sit on the front porch quiet, waiting for the other to begin the conversation. "So what's up, Victoria?"

"Kami, there is so much that I need to tell you."

"There's nothing that you can say to rectify this, Victoria." She must call her mother by her first name to insure that Victoria knows how she feels.

"I have to at least try."

"Alright, go for it."

"I'll start from the beginning. Your father and I were having problems back then and I didn't know what else to do."

"So you fake your death and leave your child all because of some shit between you and Sly?"

"Kami, I need you to listen to me, hear me out. This wasn't a small issue I was dealing with. Sly developed a drug habit and it was bad. So bad that there were drug dealers always looking for him and threatening my life as well as yours. That's how I got into selling. I had to in order to save his life and ours. I would work off his debts with the local kingpins. One of which was a man named Red."

"Sly told me that Red killed you."

"He tried. Sly got into big debt with Red and I refused to sell anything for him because he'd always try and screw me. I didn't know that Sly told him that he could have me. I was out making deliveries for another dealer when Red came up to me. He told me that I was late for our sex date. I told him that I wasn't fucking him and he became angry. He raped me, beat me and then threw me in a dumpster and left me for dead. All while his son watched."

"You met his son a while ago."

"Was it Ethan?"

"Yeah."

"He looks just like that mutha-fucka. Kami, I had to leave. I woke up in a hospital a few days after Red attacked me and I just unhooked myself from everything and caught the Greyhound to Florida. I couldn't take anymore and there was no way that I could've gone back to that house.

Sly basically signed a death certificate for me when he told Red that he could have me. I'm so sorry for what Lester did to you, but baby, I had no idea. Everyone thought that I was dead so I changed my name to Jackie Robinson and never looked back."

"Jackie Robinson?" Somehow Kamille is able to laugh at the name.

"Yep." Victoria laughs, happy to see the smile on Kamille's face.

"I thought that Ethan and Red killed you together."

"No, it was just Red."

"You should've come back for me Victoria. Do you have any idea how much I missed you? My life would be completely different."

"I thought about you everyday. There were times that I wanted to come up here and steal you in the middle of the night but I just couldn't bring myself to do it. Then years passed and I figured that you would be better off without me."

"Better off, huh? Living with my junky father, you thought I'd be better off?"

"I thought he'd take care of you."

"Huh?"

"Kami, I'm sorry, please forgive me."

"I don't know, Victoria. This is some serious shit. I've been thinking about all of this more than I've been thinking about Los. Do you have any idea how I'm feeling right now?"

"I feel like shit, Kami."

"You should. I stayed up night after night for years waiting on you to come home. I just knew that Sly was wrong and that you'd walk through that front door and hold me like you used to. Maybe we could sing and dance around the house for hours on end and enjoy each other's company. I needed to talk to you about boys and school and life. You weren't there though. All this time you were a few hundred miles away. My life was a wreck by the time I was eleven years old. I lived with a man that should've loved me and protected me, but instead he abused me." Kamille allows her tears to flow free. The pain in her heart tightens her spirit and she wants revenge.

"I was so scared and I just buried myself in this life full of regret and anger. When I heard that Sly was in jail and that you were living with your aunt Nadia, I thought everything was fine."

"Nadia kicked me out after a month. She told Lester that she couldn't afford to take care of me and that was that."

"If I had known about Lester doing those things to you I would've come back. No matter what the cost."

"How would you have known? You were dead! Who would've told you a fucking ghost or some guardian angel that I obviously didn't have?"

"I know you're angry." Victoria has her head down in shame.

"Angry? You're damn right I'm angry! I'm furious! I want to kill you, I want to kill Sly. I wish I could bring Lester back from the dead and blow his brains out myself. I want to have my life back. The life that I probably was supposed to have. The family that was supposed to love me." Kamille is hysterical now. Her speech is heavy and harsh.

Victoria leaps from her seat to hold Kamille. She allows that grown woman she left behind to cry on her shoulders. As far as she is concerned, Kamille can cry for years and she still wouldn't be able to fix her mistakes, but she'd damn sure try to mend a few of the wounds. "I'm sorry, baby." She whispers in her ear as she holds her tight. "Please forgive me."

Kamille rises while releasing herself from Victoria grasp. She wipes her face, blinks her eyes a few times and seemingly shakes off all of her frustration.

"I can try to forgive you but right now we need to go see about Red."

Kamille and Victoria ride to the Moses Funeral Home on the Westside of Atlanta where Ethan Moses Sr., better known as Red, is the sole owner of the wealthy establishment.

"Are we going to do this now, in broad daylight?" Victoria asks as they exit the car pulling down their ski mask.

"I heard that's how you roll."

"Yeah I've been known to kill a fool in the day time."

"Let's get it." Kamille is anxious to kill Red even with the sun shining. Even though her mother isn't dead, just the fact that he raped her and then tried to kill her is enough for her to take his life.

They enter the building with their 'tools' cocked and ready. Kamille has no idea what Red looks like, just that Ethan looks just like him. Therefore, she's being very careful not to shoot the wrong person. They walk through the halls quietly looking for the office or some indication as to where Red is. "There it is." Victoria points to a sign that reads, 'Office This Way'.

They stand at the half open door that has a sign reading *'Ethan Moses – Owner'*. Victoria is ready to bust in but is stopped when Kamille throws her hand up. The ladies listen and can hear two men talking on the other side of the door.

"*So what do you want me to do about it?*"
One man asks.

"*All I'm saying is that the bitch ain't dead. You do me a solid and I'll give you what you need.*"
Kamille and Victoria stare at each other in recognition of the second voice; it's Sylvester.

Victoria is so heated right now that she could literally pop. "*Why would I want to get rid of Vicky?*"

"*If she tells the cops what you did to her twenty years ago, you can go down for at least fifteen years.*"

There is silence as Red sits and thinks about his options. It's been years since he's had any dealings with this type of lifestyle, but he doesn't want to go to jail. "*What do you want for this information?*"

"*The hook-up with your son, Ethan. I want to get back in the 'game' and I need some products.*"

"*I don't know Sly. I don't deal with things like that anymore.*"

"*I understand that, but all you have to do is put in a good word for me and I'll handle the rest.*"

"*I don't think I can do it.*"

"*Look man, you owe me!*" Sylvester is becoming annoyed.

"*Owe you for what?*"

"*You were supposed to kill the bitch back then.   Now I have to deal with this shit now because you half ass did the job.*"

"*After all I did for you, you say I owe you? Please, if you didn't owe every drug dealer in Atlanta, I wouldn't have had to step in and clean up your mess. We ran the streets for years before Vicky even came along and I can't count how many favors you owe me. So don't try and throw that shit in my face.*"

"*The fact still remains the same that you need Victoria gone or else Jason's going to find out that you didn't do what he told you to do back then.*

I know you don't want that crazy ass nigga on your ass." Jason is a long-time 'drug lord' from Memphis.   He migrated to Georgia over thirty years ago when the FEDS were on his tail. Rumor has it, he used to supply Scotty back in the day and then Scotty became larger than him and the tables turned.   Jason never had the balls to go against Scotty so he fell back and took the short end of the stick. Since Red hasn't been associated with the 'game' in so long, Sylvester figures he can scare Red into taking his deal. There's no way Jason would retaliate. Not after all these years. Plus, he doesn't have the man power or the guts anymore.

"The only reason that I would be on Jason's bad side is because you lied to him. You were the one that told him that Vicky stole all of your dope and money and that's why you couldn't pay him. You put your own wife's head on a platter because you refused to own up to your own responsibility."

"Alright Red, I'll make it easy for you. I'll kill her. Okay, I'll take Victoria out; for one hundred thousand." Sylvester figures that if he can't get the drugs directly then he'll settle for cash and make his own connections.

"One hundred thousand? Are you serious? I don't have that kind of money."

"I'm sure you can get it."

"Stop bull-shitting around and get me the money to make this go away for you."

"I could just tell Jason that you lied and you're the one that smoked up all of his dope and then spent his money buying more drugs to put up your nose and in your veins."

"He wouldn't believe you for a second. Come on Red, lets' do business."

"How would you even get a hold of Vicky?"

"I know where she is."

"Where's that?"

"With our daughter, Kamille."

"Wait a minute. Kamille as in Kami?"

"Yeah, you know her?"

"*Not personally but I've heard of her. Ethan talks about her sometime. No way, Sly. The deal is a no go.*"

"*Why?*"

"*Are you kidding me? Do you know the reputation your daughter has? You want me to be responsible for the murder of that woman's mother? Seriously? That would be like walking in front of a bus going a hundred miles per hour. I would be better off just killing myself.*"

Kamille pushes the door open revealing Red sitting in his big, leather desk chair behind a huge wood desk and Sylvester seated in front of him. His eyes buck in shock of two people standing in front of him with guns aimed at his face. "There's no money here."

"We don't want your money, Red." Victoria speaks both women are furious. Kamille is shocked that her father, even ol' Sly, would do something so heinous. To frame his wife, the mother of his child and attempt to have her murdered over some drugs, disturbs the hell out of Kamille.

Sylvester turns around to see two masked intruders dressed in black. "What the hell?"

"Who are you? What do you want?" Red is hysterical, afraid that Jason has already found out about his shady work twenty years ago.

"You're a smart man, Red." Kamille states as she holds her .45 at the temple of her father's head. Sylvester recognizes his daughters' voice and fear laced with panic spreads across his body.

"What?" Victoria lifts her ski masks and Kamille is reminded of when she killed Scotty and how she wanted him to know who took his life. "Who are you?" He squints his eyes as if trying to see something that's not there.

"You don't remember me?"

"No. I don't."

"Sure you do Red."

"My name is Ethan Sr."

"Naw, your name is Red."

He stares at Victoria and all of a sudden his eyes glow with shock and disbelief. He looks over at Sylvester and notices that he's in some sort of shock. "Vicky?"

"Hi. Red."

Red can see the hate in Victoria's eyes and he knows that this won't be a pleasant ending. "It wasn't my idea Vicky, I swear."

"Thanks to big mouthed Sly, I know the whole story now."

"I can't believe you took my mother from me." Kamille looks down at the shell of a man that used to be her father.

Red's eyes buck as Kamille lifts her ski mask. The pounding from his chest can be heard from miles away.

"It was the drugs baby-girl, it wasn't me." Sylvester tries to plead his case.

"You're not high now. What is it this time that would cause you to voluntarily murder my mother?" Sylvester looks up into his daughter's eyes and sees pain. Pain from his brother that violated her. Pain from her lover that was murdered in front of her. The pain he caused her by plotting the murder of her mother. He knows that this is the end for him. His secrets are out and the two people that they involved the most are here to gain retribution.

"I don't have an answer to that, baby-girl."

"Cut the small talk, Sly. This is not a casual visit."

"If you're going to kill your own father, Kami,.do it now." Sly hangs his head.

Kamille looks over at Victoria and reads the expression on her face. "I'll let my mother do the honors."

Victoria turns her pistols' attention to Sylvester and releases six shots of rage from her 'tool'. She turns and stares at the converted thug that raped and beat her over twenty years ago. One shot pierces his heart and it's over.

"I feel that I should call Felix and apologize." Natacha states blunt in hand.

"Why? He was wrong for implying that you wanted to live some ghetto fabulous life without meaning."

"Damn, did he say all that?" They laugh.

"He may as well have said it. All that stuff you said he was shouting to you was rude as hell."

"Yeah, it was. But I think he really misunderstood what I was saying."

"Ride over there." Kamille is high as a kite. They're still smoking on one of the bags from Scotty's stash. "I mean damn, the dude just flipped out. He hasn't called or anything. I wouldn't be thinking about his ass."

"You gon' ride with me?" Kamille is disappointed that Natacha even cares.

"Now?" Kamille doesn't want to go. She's on a high that makes her want to chill in a hot tub of water while Anthony Hamilton sings to her. However, she must help with her best friend's personal affairs if asked to.

"Yeah now, you the one brought it up."

"I'm high as hell. My brain is still in an uproar from that shit with Victoria and Dallas."

"Come on, the ride will take your mind off of it."

"No, it won't."

Natacha laughs because she knows that the ride won't do anything for Kamille but give her more time to think about all the drama she's dealing with. "Come on, Kami."

"Alright." Like she could ever say no to Natacha.

"What the fuck?" Natacha is in shock. Pulling up to Felix's house they see yellow tape everywhere. No police are in sight but this is definitely a fresh crime scene. "What in the hell happened?"

"Damn, Natacha. Have you tried to call him at yet?"

"Naw, I figured he'd call me when he was ready. I'm gonna call him now"

"Maybe you shouldn't."

"Why not?"

"We don't know what's going on yet."

There's a young man standing on his steamboat porch across the street starring at them. "Do you see that dude over there?"

"Yeah, I see him." Kamille lights a cigarette and opens the car door. "Let's talk to him."

"Excuse me, sir." Natacha speaks first as they approach the young man.

"Yeah." He responds while walking down the steps.

"Do you know what happened across the street?" Natacha has sincere concern written on her face. She desperately wants to know what happened at Felix's house.

"That dude got killed over there."

"What?" Immediately Natacha's eyes fill with tears.

"Yeah, I heard the cops say that is was a robbery gone bad. They shot him in the head and took all the money he had."

"Oh my God!" Natacha can no longer hold her composure.

Kamille holds her friend escorting her back to the car. "Thank you." She says to the young man.

Back in the car Natacha tries to pull her self together. "I gotta find out who hit Felix." She's distraught but her sadness and grief have now turned into anger and revenge.

"No doubt. Let's go holla at Joe he might know something about it."

"Yeah, I heard about some big shot nigga getting popped up in Buckhead." Joe leans on Kamille's SUV with his hands in his pockets.

"I knew this guy Joe." Natacha speaks and Kamille sits back to let her friend handle business. "What else do you know?"

"How'd you know him?"

"I was dating him." She wipes her eyes.

Joe stands up straight and runs his hand over his bald head. He's upset that Bridgett didn't tell him everything like he'd thought. She forgot to mention that the 'mark' she gave him was Natacha's man. "I know Bridge mentioned going after some rich nigga and leaving him dead for fucking over her." Fuck Bridgett! She should've been upfront about everything from the beginning. Joe doesn't need to be crossing Kamille unnecessarily right now.

"Bridge!" Kamille has a light bulb affect. "Let's go, Natacha."

"What is it, Kami?" Natacha asks in the car.

"Remember I told you that Bridge asked about Felix?"

"Yeah, but that bitch wouldn't dare."

"I bet she would and I know she did. She's a dirty chick."

"Felix asked a lot of questions that night about what we did for a living. You think that bitch told him what was up?"

"I wouldn't be surprised if she did."

The ladies pull up to Bridgett's apartment and by this time Natacha is convinced that she had something to do with Felix getting killed.

They knock on the door, ring the bell and still have to wait all of five minutes for Bridgett to answer the door. "Yeah, what y'all want?" Bridgett opens the door with much attitude.

Pop! Natacha punches her square in the nose causing it to bleed profusely. "Bitch! You got some fucking balls." Natacha kicks her in the stomach while she's down.

"What in the fuck is this?" Bridgett looks over at Kamille still standing in the doorway.

"Don't look at me. You're the one that fucked up, big time."

"What did I do?"

"Bitch!" Natacha kicks her over and over again. Taking a break she asks, "why'd you have Felix killed?"

Bridgett fixes a quizzical expression on her face. "Felix?" How in the hell did they know she had something to do with him being murdered?

"Yeah bitch. I knew you wanted him but damn. It's like that?"

Kamille is not stranger to Bridgett or her deceitful ways. "How long you been fucking him?" She asks.

Natacha looks at Kamille with question. She never thought that Felix would sleep with the likes of Bridgett, but he's a man first. "You fucked him?"

"Yeah, I fucked him?" Bridgett suddenly finds her balls again. "You thought I wouldn't? The nigga wanted me and I wanted his dough. I fucked him good too. Until I caught his ass calling you, telling you how much he loves you and shit. I got pissed! He hit me and left me at the hotel, so I had to get at him."

"Bitch!" Natacha plunges onto Bridgett beating her in the face with full force, holding nothing back. Kamille pulls her off of the lying tramp.

"Wait. What happened Bridgett?"

"Keep that bitch away from me." She points to Natacha.

"Hoe, I will kill you!" Natacha tries for her again but Kamille holds her back.

"What did you do Bridge! I know you didn't take him out by yourself." Kamille is getting angrier by the second and wants answers.

"I was in some shit with Joe, so I told him that I knew a guy that he could 'hit'. He had Spook do it."

"You marked him?"

"Why not? She's mad that I fucked him. She should be glad the nigga is dead. Plus, he talked too much shit about you being such a good girl. Bullshit! I told the lame what you really do on a daily basis, but he refused to believe that shit."

Kamille responds to Bridgett's last statement. "Oh, he believed it Bridge. Every word."

"You dirty bitch." Natacha breaks free of Kamille and slaps Bridgett across the face leaving a nice hand print. Bridgett tries to fight back but she can't sustain against Natacha's quick lefts and hard rights.

"I should've killed that bitch." Natacha is still fuming with rage as they ride down I-20.

"Too many people saw us go in there. You did right by just kicking her ass. And her ass you did kick, by the way." They laugh.

"Hell yeah, I let into that hoe."

"So we know that Joe called the hit but he blamed it on Bridge. Why?"

"I don't know. The nigga shady as hell ain't no telling why he did that shit."

"I guess we need to go see Spook."

They pull up to Spooks' shop to find Ronni there helping out.

"So I see you got your chance." Kamille startles Ronni causing her to drop the bags of weed in her hand.

"Hey y'all." She speaks as she gathers her droppings.

"Where's Spook?" Natacha has no words for Ronni at this point.

"He's inside." The ladies leave Ronni to attend to her customers.

"Let me holla at you for a minute Spook." Kamille motions for him to step into the kitchen where no one seems to be working at the moment.

"What's up, Kami? Natacha?"

"Joe called a hit on a dude up in Buckhead, did you do it?" Natacha gets right to the matter at hand.

"Yeah me and Ronni did it." Spook confesses with ease since he doesn't know that any wrong has been done.

"Ronni?" Kamille questions.

"Yeah. I wanted someone with me, so I took her. She froze up and shit but it ended up okay."

"Yeah, okay for who?" Natacha asks.

Spook feels the tension in the room now. "What's up? Something wrong?"

"Yeah, that was a friend of mine you killed."

"What? I didn't know that." Spook is truly afraid at this point.

"We know you didn't Spook." Kamille cuts in.

"This is fucked up, Kami. I know who killed Felix and I can't repay the mutha-fuckas."

"It's a sticky situation, Natacha."

"He was fucking her! Can you believe he was fucking that hoe?"

"Yeah I can. A man is a man and a hoe is a hoe. When they meet there's no telling what will happen. He probably screwed her just because he could, that's how it usually works."

"Then ask me to marry him though. That's trifling as hell."

"He might have asked out of guilt or he could've really loved you."

"Fuck it."

"It'll be okay, Natacha. You'll bounce back."

"I can't kill Ronni and Spook because they didn't know who he was. But that damn Bridge, got-damn it. Am I that damn stupid, Kami?"

"No. You aren't stupid at all. You know how many women get cheated on by men they thought really loved them?"

"Yeah but not me, I should've seen this shit. I didn't even have a chance to apologize for the things I said."

"You told the truth, Natacha. You let him know how you really felt before y'all made a huge mistake." Just then Natacha's cell phone rings; unknown number.

"*Hello.*"

"*Yes, Natacha please.*"

"*This is she.*"

"Hi, this is Detective Monroe from the Atlanta Police Department." The female voice on the other end of the line introduces herself.

Natacha looks over at Kamille. "What, who is it?" She whispers.

"Okay." Natacha speaks back into the phone.

"We're investigating the homicide of a Felix Tanker and your number is in the recent calls of his cell phone. We were hoping you could come down to the station and help us piece some things together."

"Yeah, I can do that."

Natacha has Kamille drop her off at her SUV. She feels the need to do this alone.

"Detective Monroe, please." She's speaking to a female officer at the front desk in the precinct.

"You are?"

"Natacha, she's expecting me." The officer picks up the phone and delivers the message of Natacha's arrival.

"Go straight through those doors, ma'am." The officer points to a set of glass, double doors.

"Natacha, thanks for coming in. I'm Detective Sherrie Monroe." The beautiful, tall, slim, dark-skinned detective extends her hand. Natacha is taken back by her beauty; skin so fresh and dark. High cheek bones and full lips make her face timeless and flawless.

Natacha accepts her greeting, "no problem."

"Have a seat."

"Detective Monroe I don't know what I can tell you about Felix."

"Probably more than you think Ms....."

"Oats. All I know is that he was killed. I just found out myself."

"How'd you find out?"

"I hadn't heard from him in a few days so I went by his house and that's when I saw the yellow tape. I figured something horrible had happened."

"You're right about that. It seems to have been a robbery. The safe was open and empty. There also seemed to be some jewelry missing from his dresser."

"Yeah, Felix was flashy."

"What was your relationship to Mr. Tanker?"

"We dated a few years back and disassociated until recently. He contacted me about some property for sale. That's what he did, real estate investments. We began dating again after that. He wanted to get married but I was undecided."

The detective's eyes widen. "So you two were pretty close then?"

"Yeah, I guess so. I just wasn't sure if I wanted to marry him or not."

"Why's that?"

"He wasn't really my type. He treated me okay but he was a little soft."

"Soft?"

"Yeah, you know, passive."

"So you know of anyone who would want to cause harm to Mr. Tanker?"

"No, well..."

"What is it Ms. Oats? Whatever you can tell me will be greatly appreciated."

"There's this chick named Bridgett Weaver, she had a thing for Felix."

"How do you know this 'chick'?"

"Just from around the way. We were associates at one point in time but her lifestyle is a little too wild for me."

"What do you mean by that?"

"She's into street drugs and thugs. That's not my thing so I had to part ways with her. She knew that I was dating Felix and I believe they had an affair."

"Why do you think that?"

"I heard from a reliable source that they were hooking up from time to time."

"Uh-huh, so would Bridgett have any reason to hurt Felix?" Detective Monroe asks while taking notes.

"She knows a lot of people; bad people. It's possible that Felix broke it off with her and she made this whole thing happen. I heard that she got some friends of hers to do it, but I'm not sure."

"Why would they do something like this for someone like Bridgett?"

"They all use drugs and Bridgett has the connections to get them all the dope they want."

"Okay, so what are the names of the two alleged accomplices?"

"The female is Ronni Carter and she hangs with this guy named Chauncy Pearson better known as Spook. They probably did the murder for her."

"Thank you for this information, Natacha. Looks like you're pretty emotional right now. It'll be okay. We'll catch who did this."

"I hope I helped out some. Felix and I had our differences but I loved him."

Three birds with one stone. Natacha couldn't pass up the opportunity to throw some attention to the real killers. Hopefully this will get all three of them out of her life.

11

RAY & KAMI

KAMILLE IS SITTING IN A HOT TUB OF WATER JUST LETTING THE STEAM FILL THE AIR. After a day of showing the new thugs, Donta' and Rashad, how to sell their weed for a big profit, she needs a nice long bath. Donta' decided that he wants to hang with the big boys and slang a lil' of that 'hard' and Kamille has no problem opening another shop, but first she has to see how he handles 'lightweight'.

Candles are lit and Lenny Williams plays from the CD player. She goes back to the night Carlos was killed and sees him in the tub with her, he sends her a wink and she smiles. Her cell phone ringing breaks the reunion. She reaches on the side of the tub and grabs it.

"Hello."

"*Kami?*"

"*Yeah, who's this?*"

"*Ray.*"

"*Hey Ray, what's up?*"

"*Missin' you.*"

"*Is that right?*"

"*That's right. What's up wit' 'cha?*"

"*Nothin', chillin'.*"

"*I just wanted to let you know that you were on my mind.*"

"*Run that game. nigga.*"

"*That ain't game, it's the truth.*"

"*I've been thinkin' about you too.*" She touches her right nipple. Realizing what she's doing, she stops and looks around to be sure that no one in the empty house sees her.

"*Good thoughts?*"

"*Yeah.*"

"*That's what's up!*"

"*Yeah, how's everything with you?*"

"*It's all good, can't sit still though.*"

"*Yeah I know.*"

"*I need to come down that way and chill with you for a few.*"

"*Yeah you should.*"

"*Don't play, 'cause a nigga want to see ya'.*"

"*I'm not playin'. You're welcome to come chill.*"

"*When?*"

141

"*Whenever.*"

"*I'm good for the next few weeks so how about tomorrow?*"

"*That's cool. What time should I expect you?*"

"*Shit, probably 'bout two.*"

"*Cool.*"

"Come on in." Kamille snatches the front door open and runs to the kitchen.

"What's up?" Ray closes the door and follows her.

"I was smokin' and fell asleep. I forgot I had a pizza in the oven."

Ray fans smoke from his face. "Don't tell me you can't cook." He laughs.

"Yeah a little, but I dozed off." Kamille takes the pizza out of the oven and places the burnt lunch on the stove. "Damn."

"You want to go get something to eat?"

"Yeah." She looks up at Ray. "You look good."

"Not me baby, you."

"Hum. You want some pizza? Not this one, but I'll order one."

"Yeah that's cool."

They sit and smoke blunt after blunt and then gobble down the large supreme pizza.

142

"What's good ma'?" Ray asks as they sit watching BET in the living room.

"Nothing." Kamille sighs. "Absolutely nothing."

Ray scoots over to be closer to her and puts his arm around her waist. "What's wrong?"

"Everything."

"Talk."

"Joe's trying to kill me."

"What?"

"He's the one who killed Los and who's been sending folks after me."

"But that's yo' home-boy, ain't he?"

"Was."

"What the fuck is this nigga thinking?"

"He got greedy."

Ray asks an obvious question. "So when you gon' pop 'em?"

"Soon, I just don't know if he has my workers on his side or not. I don't know who I can trust."

"You can trust me." He rubs his hand across her face.

"I know." Kamille gets up. "I'm gonna go take a shower."

"Okay."

"You want to join me?"

Ray looks up at her and smiles. "Yeah I do."

"Come on."

Kamille and Ray shower together, bathing and caressing each other with care and maybe even a little love. She's a little tense at first, since she's never willingly made love to another man. Plus this is the last space she'd shared with Carlos. However, the more Ray kisses and touches her, the more comfortable she becomes. They make love and then bathe each other again.

Kamille dries off and throws her towel across the bed and begins to search for something comfortable yet sexy to put on.

"Can I get a lil' more of that?" Ray asks as he stands in the door-way of the bathroom.

"If you want it, come get it." She meets him half way and they kiss hard and Ray pushes her down on the bed.

"Open up." He eases down on her, kissing her neck and making his way down to her lake of fire. He tastes her and savors every drop. Kamille can't hold back the moans; it's been so long since she let a man enter her space, not to mention Ray is just the second. She thinks to her self how different he is from Carlos, in a good way. Carlos satisfied her but Ray has a thug-ness that just over takes her and causes every womanly urge to come forth.

Kamille moves her hips, pushing her pussy deeper into Rays' face. He slurps and nibbles on her clit. She pulls the pillow from behind her and smothers her own face. Ray pulls it away.

"I want to hear you moan for me, Kami." She does as he wishes and allows her cries to fill the air and suffocate the atmosphere.

"Ray, can you do me a favor?" Kamille asks as she lies on his naked chest.

"Anything, Ma'." The way she makes him feel, he'll gladly stand buck naked in fire for her right now.

"Is it possible for you to put word out not to sell to Joe."

"What do you mean?"

"I mean you and Ace stop selling to him and tell who ever you know to do the same."

"Yeah, I guess so. We could say that he's in some shit and made a deal with the FEDS."

"Good, do that for me. I don't want this nigga to be able to get shit."

"Done deal." He kisses her forehead and then pulls her on top of him for another round.

"Hey, Ray." Natacha speaks as she enters Kamille's house.

"What's good?"

"I can't even answer that." She responds as she makes her way to the kitchen. "What's up, Kami?"

"Hey, boo."

"Boo? Umm, you must've got some."

Kamille laughs and turns to face her friend. "Yep and it was gooood."

"I can hear y'all." Ray shouts from the living room.

The ladies break out in laughter again. It's something that they both need. They are as they were as young girls. Back when they didn't have a care in the world. Before they were dealt the hand they'd have to play in the game of life.

Natacha continues. "Alright, so you called me over here to gloat?"

"Naw, I need to give you something."

"What?" Kamille hands her a small piece of paper with a series of numbers written on it. "What's this?"

Knowing that Ray now has supernatural ears, Kamille breaks to a whisper. "It's the combination to my safe at the airport. It has all my money in it and my 'will'."

"Why are you giving me this?"

"Just in case something happens to me. I need you to promise me something."

"Wait a minute Kami. What in the hell is going on?"

"Nothing, it's just *in case* Natacha."

Natacha sighs and rubs her temples. "I was combing my hair this morning and I saw two gray strands."

"Natacha.""I can't take this shit. All these mutha-fuckas turning they backs on us and now you talking about yo' fuckin' will. I can't do this shit, Kami."

"Listen, I don't need you breaking down on me now. This shit is just precaution. I just need you to promise that you'll take care of Tashjma if I'm not here. There's more than enough money to cover any and everything you'll need or think you'll need. I want Tashjma to go to college. She promised me that she will, there's money for that too."

"Got-damn itm, Kami." Natacha throws her hands over her ears.

"Listen." Kamille pulls her friend to her and hugs her. "I just want to make sure that y'all are okay, that's all."

"Whatever, Kami. Yeah, I'll take care of yo' foster child."

"Alright, that's all I ask. Oh yeah, I have a million dollar life insurance policy and you're the beneficiary."

"Damn right I am." They laugh.

"You know?"

"Yeah I saw it on your dresser a long time ago."

"Alright. I heard that Ronni and Spook got arrested for the murder of Felix."

"For real?" Natacha is happy to hear this news.

"Yeah, Nard says that Ronni was so high when they arrested her that she confessed to everything."

"Good."

"They didn't get Bridge though." Kamille fixes a quizzical look on her face.

Natacha is confused as well. "Why?"

"I don't know. Nard says that she definitely got questioned at her apartment and down at the station."

"Why wouldn't they arrest her?"

"All I can think of is that she have given them something else they've been wanting."

"Like what?"

"Me."

"What?" Natacha stares at her friend in disbelief.

"They'd been after Los for years. I know that the FEDS have been trying to figure out who's taken his place."

"You think they've been watching you."

"I can feel it."

"Damn! I'm so fuckin' stupid!"

"No, you're not."

"Yes I am. If hadn't gone down there and snitched on that bitch then this wouldn't be happening."

"It's inevitable, Natacha. No matter what Bridge told them about me, they can't prove a damn thing. This shit is wrapped so tight that I could fart and the FEDS wouldn't smell it. Don't worry baby, it's all good."

12

A *FEW WEEKS PASS AND EVERYTHING IS SERENE.* No murders or threats. Life couldn't be better for Kamille and her team. Joe has even shopped with Kamille a few times, trying to make things seem cool.

Life is too good right now. Natacha thinks about this as she lets the hot water flow over her body in the shower. Stress screams from her muscles and runs down the drain. She can smell the fresh scent of marijuana as her previously lit blunt sits in the ashtray in the window seal. She thinks of how much she wants to get out of the 'game'. Finally seeing what Kamille has been talking about; this life is foul. Love found and then taken away in the blink of an eye over senseless bullshit. Making deals and breaking laws. Watching your back just because you're successful at what you do but shady mutha-fuckas want to see you dead.

Natacha steps out of the shower just in time to catch her cell phone ringing.

"*Hello.*"

"*What it do, boo?*" Kamille plays around with some Ebonics with her friend.

"*Nothing psycho. What are you doing?*"

"*Smoking, thinking about life.*"

"*Oh shit, you got you some of that mind twisting weed. Shit, be having you thinking hard as hell.*" They laugh at the true statement.

"*I just have a lot on my mind. Ray is getting ready to leave.*"

"*Awww! Your man leaving town has you down.*" Natacha laughs at the expense of her friend. Kamille will miss Ray like crazy. When she's with him she doesn't think about Carlos. Ray has such a different vibe about his self. She's fallen in love with him."

"*Shut up, bitch!*"

"*I'm just playing, Kami. I know you're going to miss him. He'll be back soon though, don't worry over it.*"

"*He'll be in town for the rest of the day. It's no biggie.*"

"*He has work in the 'A'?*"

"*Yeah.*"

"*Alright well we need to keep you busy. Let's go check on the shops, see what's going on.*"

"*The shops are fine. Everything is going too well.*"

"*I was thinking the same thing. But that's good, right?*"

"*It's always quiet before the storm. I'll come pick you up. We can ride through if you want to.*"

"*Okay.*" Natacha flips her phone closed and thinks out loud, '*quiet before the storm.*'

Natacha exits her apartment building full speed, rushing for no reason at all, just feeling rushed. She's lugging a huge, black trash bag full of clothes that she wants to give to Tashjma. Unlocking her SUV from the keypad and reaching to open the door she hears a call of her name, "excuse me, Ms. Oates." Natacha turns to see Detective Monroe walking towards her with a man a few steps behind.

"Detective Monroe?"

"Yes ma'am. How are you this fine day?"

"I'm good." Natacha waits for whatever is coming next.

"This is Detective Sunday from the Atlanta Police Narcotics Unit." She gestures to the short, stout, Caucasian man now standing beside her.

"Hi."

"Hello, Natacha." There are a few seconds of silence filled with tension that can't be cut with the sharpest blade.

"How can I help you guys today?" Natacha speaks with smooth and even tone; showing no sign of fear or intimidation. The word Narcotics keeps ringing in her head.

Detective Monroe speaks first. "Well we've joined up to investigate a string of murders, missing persons and drug trafficking."

"Okay."

"Recently it has come to our attention that you may be involved in the cases that we're working."

"Seriously?" Natacha pretends to be confused.

Detective Sunday sticks his hands into his pockets and leans against Natacha's SUV. "We have reason to believe that you are part of a drug cartel ran by a woman by the name of Kamille Lathan."

Natacha lets out a laugh. "You got this from Bridgett right?" She asks the question to Detective Monroe.

"We've been watching Ms. Lathan for a while now." Detective Sunday answers, but Natacha knows that it's a lie. If they'd been watching Kamille they would've arrested her by now.

"What does that have to do with me?"

Detective Monroe takes this one. "We know that you two are close. We also know that you play a large role in her operation."

Natacha laughs again. "Her operation?"

"That's right." There's no smile on Detective Monroe's face.

"I don't know what Bridgett told y'all to make sure that she doesn't go to jail for plotting the murder of Felix, but this is ridiculous. Kamille is not a part of any operation and neither am I."

Detective Sunday rubs his left temple and sighs. "Are you familiar with a man by the name of Carlos Higgins?" Agitation shows on his face as he stares at Natacha waiting for a response.

"Yes, I am." Natacha answers with ease knowing very well that they know that Carlos is dead. Both detectives glare at her waiting for any sign of weakness or fear. Nothing.

Kamille slowly drives through the apartment complex. She sees Natacha standing at her SUV speaking with two unknown individuals who look much like cops. She parks a few building away and waits. There no movement just conversation. Natacha looks relaxed but she knows that's a front. Surely these two are some kind of officers but what sort, Kamille is unaware. She picks up her phone and places a call to Natacha.

"Hello."

"Everything good?"

"I'm not sure."

"I'm coming over."

"That's not necessary."

"We ride together, Natacha." She hangs up.

"Is there anything else, detectives?" Natacha asks. She doesn't want Kamille to get involved no matter what she says.

"We know that Kamille was Carlos' companion." Detective Sunday shares the already known information.

"Yes, I was." Both detectives turn to see Kamille standing behind them. "I would rather be present if I'm being spoken about."

Detective Monroe glares at Natacha knowing that she must've been who she was talking to on the phone. "We're actually very happy that you're here, Ms. Lathan." She extends her hand. "I'm Detective Monroe. Kamille doesn't accept so Detective Monroe lowers her greeting back to her side.

Natacha knows how her friend feels about the police so she feels the need to intervene before things get out of hand. "Detective Monroe works homicide and this is Detective Sunday from narcotics."

Kamille doesn't budge. She has her stare locked on Detective Monroe and the detective returns the same. Kamille doesn't like this woman. The vibe she gets from her reeks of someone that wants to see her buried. "We know a lot about you Kamille." Detective Sunday speaks breaking the mental war between Kamille and Detective Monroe.

"Meaning?"

"Meaning we know what type of life Carlos led and we know that you took over after his death."

"Is that right?"

"Yes it is?" Detective Monroe cuts back in.

"I don't know where all of this is coming from all of a sudden but I am in no way affiliated with any business Carlos conducted.

"Our sources seem to tell us differently."

"Then I suggest you find other sources."

Detective Sunday steps in to try and divert the ladies confidence. "You've been doing quit a bit of shopping Ms. Lathan. Expensive cars, new house, splurging in Buckhead, Lenox and Phipps, the list can go on and on."

"I didn't know there was a law against fine living, Detective Sunday."

'Oh there isn't, but there are laws against murder and distribution of narcotics."

"Murder? Narcotics? This is insane. Not that it's either of your business but I was the beneficiary of Carlos' insurance policy. Plus, he owned a house that was left to me and I sold it. That's where the money is coming from. Just to put your minds at ease."

"So you didn't sell your house because too many drug dealers knew where you lived?"

"Let me educate you on something, Detective Sunday. We all know what Carlos did for a living, that's no secret, but because of who he was, I do not have to be afraid of anyone. Whether they be drug dealers or not. I sold my house because of the memories of Carlos, nothing else is relevant." That statement is true. Kamille couldn't stand being in that place knowing that Carlos would never walk through the doors again. "See detectives, I don't have to be afraid of anything, I have nothing to hide. Now as much as I'd love to continue this soiree, I have more important matters to attend to."

"What happened to Scott Farmer?" Detective Monroe throws a low blow. "Word in the street is that he had Carlos killed and then you had him killed."

"Scott Farmer?" Kamille pretends to be confused.

"Yeah you know Mr. Farmer. Carlos worked for him. They call him Scotty."

"Sorry, don't know him."

"Sure you do." Detective Sunday assures. "It's okay. We appreciate all you do to clean up the community. One way or another you'll have to pay for it though."

"Goodbye detectives." Kamille turns to walk away.

"One more thing, Ms. Lathan." Detective Sunday continues. "A couple of my agents were killed a little while ago in a grenade attack. Would you know anything about that?" He attempts his tactic of trying to scare Kamille again.

"Why would I?"

"It's unconfirmed, but they may have been tailing you when they were killed."

"I'm not in the business of killing Detective and I don't know anything about grenades or any other weapons you plan on conjuring up."

"So you're not familiar with firearms either?"

"Not in the least bit." She turns and walks away towards her SUV.

"We'll be watching you Ms. Lathan." Kamille throws her hand in the air giving the officers a peace sign. Natacha gets into her Jeep as well and drives off. Natacha knows not to leave her vehicle there, just in case the detectives want to do an illegal search.

Natacha follows Kamille to a restaurant a few miles from the apartment. Once they part

Natacha gets out of her Jeep and hops into Kamille's SUV. "What in the hell, Kami?"

"This shit is crazy." Kamille lights a cigarette.

"This is all my fault." Natach grabs Kamille cigarette box and lights one of her own. The thought of doing jail time scares the living hell out of her.

"Why do you say that?"

"I should've never went to rat out Bridge. That lady detective is the same one that I talked to about Felix."

"Damn."

"I'm sorry."

"Naw, forget about that. You did what you felt you had to do. That damn Bridge is the one who's running her mouth. Jealousy is a beast."

"Hell yeah. We have to get rid of that chick."

"Yeah, we do."

"Damn, Kami. We have to lay low for real now that they think it was us that killed those 'Narcs'."

"Yeah, but they weren't supposed to be in that area anyway. No one knew that they were following me."

"Why would they do that and not be assigned to?"

"That's my question."

13

IT'S THREE O'CLOCK IN THE MORNING AND KAMILLE IS AWAKENED BY THE SOUND OF GLASS BREAKING. At first she thinks that it's Tashjma messing something up but then she remembers that she spent the night with Natacha. She reaches under her bed and pulls out her 12 gauge shotgun, then pulls her faithful .45 from under her pillow and screws the silencer on. She makes her way down the hall on her tiptoes and freezes when she hears the sound of footsteps coming from her living room. She thinks to her self how stupid it was to let Ray leave just a few hours before even though he wanted so badly to stay. But she figured that they had done enough sucking and fucking and she doesn't want them to get tired of each other so early in the situation.

"Who's in my house?" She screams out, ready for whatever.

"It's the 'grim-reaper' bitch." A voice, unfamiliar, shoots back.

Kamille dips around the corner leading to the side entrance of the kitchen. She sees no one and decides that she'll steak-out there. She peeps over the bar and sees one figure dressed in all black, but his head is turned and she can't see his face, too skinny to be Joe, she thinks to her self. Just then a shadow begins to surface coming from the living room and into the kitchen. She gets her shotgun ready and aims for the intruder's head. The guy is walking backwards as if he's expecting her to come from the hallway and he should, being that the side door to the kitchen is unseen from the front door. She lowers the 12 gauge and waits for him to get close enough to her and far enough from the living room and puts the .45 to his head.

"Hands up, mutha-fucka." She whispers. The burglar does as he is told and she grabs the pistol from his grip. Swinging him around, Kamille bucks her eyes in shock. "Coupe?"

"I had no choice, Kami. It was kill you or get killed." She snatches his gun from his grip. No need to ask him who sent him and she doesn't even want any more information. Just the thought that her boy, from way back, would be the one called to her death. That's fucked up! Kamille squeezed the trigger and Coupe's body hit the floor, hard. She drops his pistol, puts her .45 in her shorts and puts the gauge up at full attention. Running out of the kitchen she unloads on the dude still standing in her living room and one in her hall way.

"Any more of you mutha-fuckas want some of Kami?" No answer. "Huh?" Still no answer. "Punk mutha-fucka knows that he gotta send some real fuckin' soldiers after me, Sending these half dick mutha-fuckas to do a true bitches' job."

Kamille walks over to the dark figure lying dead in the hallway, Traz. "Ain't this some shit!" She thinks out loud. "This mutha-fucka using *my* niggas!"

She drags Coupe, Traz and the third unknown out the back door and to the back yard. She drags them as far back as she can and places them one on top of the other. Going back into the house she grabs a gas can from the garage and a box of matches.

Kamille stands at a distance and watches the flesh burn and the thick black smoke fill the sky. The odor of burning flesh makes her gage and she throws up a little.

"Kamille." Kamille turns around and can see a short, hunched over shadow near the house. She begins to walk towards it.

"Mrs. Fletcher?"

"Yeah baby. What 'chu doing out here this time of morning?"

"Burning leaves."

"Don't smell like no leaves."

"They've been back there so long and I think a possum or something was in the midst of 'em."

"Oh okay. I heard a lot of commotion and I swore I heard banging noises. You know, like gunshots."

"Really. I haven't heard anything."

"What's that on your shirt?"

Damn, she forgot that blood is splattered all over her. Good thing it's dark outside. "Oh, it's nothing. I'm washing so I just grabbed one of my old sleep sets, it's just some dried paint."

"Looks like something's on your face too. Well, okay, well soon as them leaves die down, you get in the house. I'ma go 'cause it's a little too nippy out here for me."

"Yes ma'am."

Kamille goes back into the house and begins to scrub her floors to get rid of the bloodstains. She opens the windows so that her home can air out. A few tears flow down her face and she can't help but to have her very first breakdown. Kamille slides down the hall way wall and lands on the floor with her knees bent into her chest. She wraps herself in her own arms and rocks back and forth. 'I'm so tired of this.' She cries out to dead air. She grabs her cordless phone and calls the only man that she knows she can trust.

"*Ray, you hit the road yet?*" Kamille calls for protection.

"*Naw, I'm over here on Bankhead making some drops*"

"*Come back over here, please.*"

"*Fo' sho' baby, what's up?*"

"*That nigga just tried again.*" She states inhaling on her cigarette.

"This is bullshit, Kami. I'm staying here with you tonight." Natacha states sitting on the sofa blunt in hand.

"Naw, there's no need for that." It's the next day and Kamille had to call her friend and tell her what was up. Natacha filled Tashjma in on the facts and the two ladies hurried to Kamille's aid. "Ray stayed last night and I don't think Joe will try to kill me two nights straight."

"Fuck that shit, Kami. That nigga wants you dead and looks like he's getting real damn restless." Natacha is pissed. She goes to the refrigerator and grabs a bottled Corona.

"I gotta get this nigga quick."

"I don't understand what the fuck the hold up is."

"Two of the dudes I took out last night were Coupe and Traz." Kamille has tears in her eyes.

"Get the fuck outta here." Natacha's mouth falls wide open in disbelief.

"You loved 'em, Kami?" Tashjma asks referring to the tears.

"Yeah I did, but these tears are of anger baby. I'm so fuckin' mad I could go blow that bitch up right now. The thing is I don't know what will happen after that. This nigga probably got bills on my head plus I think he has cops on his payroll."

"Why do you say that?"

"That's the only explanation for the Narc detective not knowing about those cops tailing me."

"Hell yeah. They were definitely doing that shit on the side." Natacha agrees. "What we gon' do Kami?"

"I don't know. Ray got work in North Atlanta tonight, but I'm not scared to stay here. That nigga isn't going to put me out of my house."

"Well, I'm staying here with you and you can't tell me no 'cause I live here." Tashjma says very sternly. Kamille gives Tashjma a loving smile. Even though this isn't the life she'd want for her own children, she can't help but to be proud of Tashjma and her loyalty.

"You sure you alright?" Ray asks Kamille as they get out of the shower.

"Yeah, I'm cool."

"Just ride with me."

"Naw, I'm cool Ray. Just go and get back as soon as you can."

"Alright, but I don't like this shit. I need to be with you."

"I don't want anything to happen to you too. Just go."

"Why in the fuck are you giving up?" Ray stands strong over Kamille, looking down at her in frustration.

"I'm not giving up I just know when my luck has run out." Kamille even surprises herself with the statement. She questions her place in the 'game'. Is she afraid of Joe? Maybe so or maybe she's afraid of the power that he holds. But doesn't she hold the same rank if not higher?

"Ain't shit ran out. That mutha-fucka ain't shit."

"I know Ray."

Kamille decides that she and Tashjma will take a ride for a while until Ray gets back. Even though she said that she's not scared, truth be told, she's scared shitless. She looks over at the dresser and notices that Ray left his door key. Earlier today she went to the key shop and had a copy made, just in case he needed to come to the house and she wasn't there. She grabs the key, sticks it in her pocket and throws on a jacket.

"Come on, Tashjma. We're going to ride out for a minute." She says going down the hall way and calling Rays' cell phone at the same time.

Kamille comes to a halt as she stares at Tashjma bound by rope in a chair in the living room, mouth tapped and crying.

"What the fuck?"

"Hey, Kami." Joe comes from the kitchen and Kamille sees that he's not alone. "Nigga, you better be ready."

Joe smirks and two other guys walk out from the kitchen with Bridgett right behind them.

"I'm ready, Kami. Are you?"

"Fuck you, nigga!"

He smirks again. "Why in the fuck wouldn't you just chill the fuck out, Ma'?"

"Why in the fuck did you kill Los?"

"The mutha-fucka was in the way." His voice rises. "I built this shit! That nigga didn't know shit about being the ringleader. I showed and taught that nigga everything he knew and then you try and take over what I fuckin' built. You caused too much shit, Kami. Giving me orders? That's bullshit! You held it down, I'll admit that, but yo' term is over, time to step down."

"You're a punk, bitch ass nigga! Why the fuck didn't you just come to me with this shit?"

"Shit, I already don' in yo' ol' man. What the fuck use are you? I tried to get wit' 'cha, let you be behind me, but naw, you wanted all this shit to yo' self. You know the company you keep is a lot like you, stubborn mutha-fucka. Too bad that little old lady next door wouldn't mind her own business."

"What?"

"She came over, I told her to go back home. She wanted to know what we were doing over here at your back patio door. She wouldn't leave so I had to pop her."

"You killed a helpless old lady?" Kamille thinks of Mrs. Fletcher and has to fight back the tears.

"Look got-damn it, she was hard of fuckin' hearing or something 'cause I told the bitch to dip and she wanted to stay, so I had to dismiss her ass."

Kamille looks over at Tashjma. "Let her go."

"Who her?" He points to Tashjma. "Hell naw, she's the reason yo' ass put all this together. What are the odds that you'd take in a little bitch that knows about me and my plan? Things were in yo' favor for a minute Kami, but the tables have turned baby and this shit gotta end."

"Let me kill her." Bridgett comes from behind the entourage. Kamille looks at her in disgust. "What? Surprised to see me? Thought I'd still be in jail? The police didn't have shit on me with Felix. Plus, I gave you up. You may as well die 'cause the FEDS gon' put you under the damn jail."

"You're a stupid bitch and you've always been stupid." Kamille means every word.

"Fuck you!" Bridgett walks towards Tashjma and pulls out a pocket knife.

"You better not fuck with her."

"You care more about this lil' chick than you do me and you just met the girl." She puts the knife to Tashjma's face and slices. Tashjma's screams are heard through the tape covering her mouth.

"Bitch!" Kamille grabs the lamp sitting on the end table near her and busts the dude behind her in the face, pulls her .45 from her back and pops the next one standing closes to her. She moves quickly to shoot Joe, but she's too slow. She gets met with his Beretta and receives two quick shots to the chest.

As Kamille lay face down, Bridgett continues slicing and dicing on Tashjma, having her fun. The only one left from Joe's crew, besides Bridgett, gets a gas tank and begins dousing the house. Tashjma has passed out from the incisions and Joe leaves his fallen goons behind to parish.

"Burn this shit down." Joe orders as if the process wasn't already underway.

14

"**M**AN, WHAT DO YOU MEAN YOU AIN'T GOT NOTHING FOR ME YO'?"

"Just what I said. I ain't got shit for you." Joe is pissed that this is his sixth connect and he's been unable to purchase any drugs for distribution. None of his folks will sell to him or give him another connect. He needs tons of cocaine, crack, marijuana and ecstasy pills. Joe's workers are beyond low on products and their regular junkies are beginning to shop elsewhere.

"What the fuck is going on yo?"

"Ay nigga, it's out 'bout yo' ass. Everybody knows what's up so get the hell outta here."

"Everybody knows what?" Joe doesn't understand.

"Get the fuck out, nigga." The former connect raises his .45 to Joe and the room full of outlaws do the same.

"I don't know what the hell is going on?"

"What's wrong with you, baby?" Bridgett asks her faithful man.

"I been to six 'connects' and they ain't workin' with me."

"Why not?"

"That's what I don't know. This shit has been going on for months now and it's drying up 'round here."

"It'll be okay. baby." She tries to touch him but he jerks away.

"Get off me, yo'."

"Damn, Joe."

"Ay, shit is getting tight and until I get some work, yo' ass gon' have to do something."

"Do something like what?"

"Go back to yo' former job. You know what's up. I'm hungry and so are my boys. we need money coming in until I find a connect."

"Aww man, fuck that."

He grabs her by the hair. "What the fuck did you say?"

"Why I gotta go back to the strip club 'cause you can't find no work?"

Smack!! He slaps her over and over again until blood runs down her face and on to her six hundred dollar Gucci sweater. "Now you gon' take yo' ass back to that club and shack yo' shit to them horny dudes and bring me some dough. Understand?"

"Yeah." She pauses to think about what just happened.

"*I don't know what else to do, Ace.*" Natacha pours out her heart to the only one that really understands.

"*I know baby, but you gotta try and move on.*"

"*Move on? I can't move on, my best friend is dead. I mean she left me straight, real straight, but I can't even do some of the shit she wanted me to do 'cause a lot of it was for Tashjma and she's dead too. I ain't got no life. There's nothing left for me.*"

"*I'm here.*"

"*Nigga, you're hundreds of miles away.*"

"*Yeah, but I can be there when you need me.*"

"*I know. I just need time to deal with all of this shit.*"

"*Natacha, I can be there in a few hours.*" Ace offers his comfort again.

"*I know you can. It's okay, I'm just frustrated. Shit just ain't the same without my girl here.*"

"*Yeah, I know.*"

"*Shit, my girl didn't even get a proper burial and plus I didn't get a chance to say goodbye. I don't even know what the hell really happened. I went down to the police station and they said that they never could make any definite IDs 'cause the three folks in the house were burned beyond recognition and they couldn't even do dental records on one of them. To top it off, the other day I get this check in the mail from her insurance company. I had forgot all about her naming me as the beneficiary. So the shit didn't add up, so I went back to the police station and asked how could she have a death certificate if they couldn't ID the bodies? They said that they don't deal with that. What kind of bullshit answer is that? Yo boy Ray won't return my calls either.*"

"*I don't think he want to get his face out there with all this shit going on. Wait 'til the heat dies out some, he'll call you.*"

"*The most fucked up part is that nigga Joe still walking 'round this mutha-fucka like shit is all gravy. If I could, I'd pop that nigga. I just ain't got the heart like Kami had. All my 'balls' came from being around her, now that she's gone, I just ain't got the urge anymore. Plus, if I kill him, niggas will be on my ass fo' sho'.*""*You don't need to. That nigga gon' get his one day. Look, why don't I just come down there?*"

"*Yeah, that would be nice.*"

174

15

BROWN BUTTER IS PACKED TO CAPAPACITY. IT'S SATURDAY NIGHT AND THE NIGGAS ARE WILLING TO PAY A BUCK TO SEE THESE HOES SHAKE THEIR ASSES. Bridgett did as she was told and went back to her old job. The job Kamille helped her to get away from. But she's back at it again, again at the hands of a nigga.

"Give it up fellas for one of yo' favorites, Bridge." The announcer makes the call and there she is, Bridgett, dressed to impress and make her man some serious dough. Nothing like he's use to but enough to get by until things tighten up.

Bridgett takes the stage dancing to a Lil John song and the dollars start flying. She swings her hips, shakes her ass, pops her pussy in a few niggas faces and bends over for some old nigga to put a dollar in her g-string. She unsnaps her bra and lets her titties hang in free space, lifting them to lick her nipples and turn the heat on some of these money grubbing niggas. She bends over to slowly and seductively remove her g-string and glances to the left to give some sexy eye contact to an unsuspecting victim. Suddenly she jumps in her skin, bucks her eyes and runs off stage.

As the crowd boo's and begin to get in array, Joe busts backstage to confront his hoe.

"What the fuck is wrong with you?"

"Kami is out there."

"What?" Joe goes back to the showroom and looks around, unsure if he's over looking important eye visuals, he walks the room giving it a thorough over look. Back in the dressing room he says, "look, I don't know what's wrong with you but ain't no females out there."

"I saw her. She had on a black sweatshirt with a hood."

"Bullshit."

"I saw her, Joe."

"You ain't seen shit. That bitch is dead. Now pull yo' shit together and get the fuck back out there."

"Alright, you right."

The owner walks in. "What's up, Joe?"

"She alright, just spooked on some shit. She'll be out there in a minute."

"Alright man, I can't have this shit going on in my club."

"She comin', yo'." The owner leaves the dressing room and Joe turns his attention back to Bridgett. "Hurry the fuck up, Bridge." He leaves to go back to the crap table.

Bridgett stands in the mirror attempting to pull her self together. *'Alright Bridge, come on girl, you trippin'.'* She thinks out loud.

"You always have been a dumb bitch." Bridgett turns around already familiar with the voice. Sure enough there she stands, Kamille in the flesh; black sweatshirt with hood.

"What the fuck?" Bridgett takes a few steps as if to run. Kamille lifts the .45 with silencer.

"Bitch, please."

"What the fuck do you want, Kami?"

"Your life. Now have a seat." Bridgett sits at one of the make-up stations, shivering.

"It wasn't me. It was Joe."

"It was you bitch. As much as I was there for you."

"You was there when it was convenient for you. Everybody came before me; Natacha, Los, Joe, even that lil' bitch Tashjma. You ain't never put me first."

"That's because I always knew you were a triflin' bitch. I just felt sorry fo' yo' ass. You know

177

what? Fuck all that, this shit is way past due."
Kamille pulls out her pocketknife, tucks her .45 in
the waist line of her pants, places her hand over
Bridgett's mouth and returns the favor. The
muffled screams went unheard, drowned out by
the ghetto lyrics coming from the show room.
Knocks and bangs come from the door.

"Hey, unlock the door." A female voice
yells.

Kamille pops two quick shots in Bridgett's
skull and turns her around to the make-up table,
head down.

"Man, where in the hell is Bridge?" Joe
asks out loud getting ready to go get her.

"Fuck her, man. They got Fantastic Tits on
stage now." One of his buddies throws his
attention to the stage.

"Damn, she do got some nice ass titties."

After fifteen minutes of watching the perfect
titties bounce on stage, the Patrone has gotten to
Joe. "I gotta go piss nigga, I'll be back yo'."

"Whew! That shit run through a nigga."
He speaks out loud as he releases himself in the
men's room. Just then the door swings open and
Joe turns to look, but the person has turned their
back. He looks at the enterers shape and declares

that it can't be a man. "Yo' miss, you hit the wrong door."

"Naw, I got it right." The woman turns and Joe's mouth drops open. Kamille lifts the .45 and walks close enough to him so that he wouldn't be unsure that it is most definitely her. She pulls her hood down off of her head to give a clear view. "I'm not gonna waste time, Joe. You know what this is."

"Ethan started all this shit."

"What?"

"That nigga Ethan, he did this shit yo'." Kamille lets out six shots and stays until Joe's body slides down the wall and his dead eyes stare back at her. Jadakiss said it best; *'you deserve it whenever you die with your eyes open'*.

"So we gonna go see about this nigga?" Ray is anxious to get rid of all Kamille's enemies. He wants to start a new life with his new found love. They can't be happy with hits out on them.

"Why would Ethan kill Los?"

"I don't know, but it's worth looking into."

Kamille and Ray arrive at Ethan's penthouse and enter through the front door. They approach the round doorman to gain entry. "We're here to see Ethan Moses." Kamille speaks to the man.

"Okay, I can call him for you."

"No thanks, we'll find him ourselves." Ray raises his 'tool' for the doorman to see.

"Whoa! No need for that sir. Mr. Moses is on the top floor, suite number eleven. But he has company; female company." The fat man gives Ethan's location with his arms raised in surrender. He's a hard working brother with little going for him but dying in the lobby of this high rise is not on his agenda. Besides Ethan has never been too nice to him anyway.

They ride the elevator up to the thirty-second floor while loading their guns on the way. They exit looking for the penthouse marked eleven. They find it before long and Ray takes charge by blowing the lock off the door. "Damn baby, can we make a more hushed entrance?"

"Hell naw."

They enter the lavish living area, guns drawn and ready for whatever. After searching the entire place, there's no sign of Ethan. "Let's check the roof."

"The roof? Why in the hell would he be on the roof?"

"He says he likes to go up there."

"Did you fuck this nigga?"

"What?"

"You heard me, Kami."

"I can't believe you asked me that and now."

"Did you?"

"No, I didn't."

"Okay."

They reach the roof to find Ethan there with a young lady that is not familiar to Kamille. They sit at a table made up with all the fixings of an Ethan's getting fucked dinner. The same dinner he would've made for her if she'd accepted his invitation. "Hey E, got a minute." Ethan turns in his seat, startled by the presence of others on *his* roof, interrupting *his* dinner.

"What the fuck?" Shocked to see Kamille standing there, he gets up from his chair in a panic.

"Sit down mutha-fucka." Ray orders with his .45 aimed and Ethan does as told.

"Surprised?" Kamille asks.

"Yeah, I thought you were dead. It's good to see that I was wrong though." He lies.

"Sure it is."

"What's up, Kami? Why do I feel like this is an ambush?"

"Shawty, you might want to leave." Kamille speaks to the young lady accompanying Ethan.

"Why?" Ethan asks. "What's up, Kami? I thought we did good business together."

"Me too." She looks at the woman again, this time waiting for her to take heed to the warning.

"Wait for me in the penthouse, baby." Ethan knows that whatever is about to happen, she doesn't need to see.

Kamille takes the vacant seat, crosses her legs and asks the million dollar question. "Did you have anything to do with killing Los?"

"What? Hell naw."

"Joe says otherwise."

"Joe?"

"Yeah, right before I killed him, he said that this was all your idea."

"Joe is dead?"

"Yep. You seem upset by that bit of information Ethan."

"He was cool. Why'd you kill him?"

"Because he tried to kill me."

"What?" Ethan tries to act surprised but fails.

"This nigga full of shit." Ray speaks while trying to resist putting a hole in Ethan's head.

"Nigga who are you?"

"Fuck you nigga, don't worry about it."

"Who is this Kami?"

"The man who's going to kill you."

"What?"

"Kami, I ain't had shit to do with this."

"Then why would your name come up? Better yet, fuck that; I know you had something to do with it. But I bet you don't know who killed your father."

"What?"

"I know E. I know who killed that mutha-fucka you call daddy."

Ethan gives a knowing stare. "Why?"

"Oh, not me, but I was there." Kamille is loving this.

"Fuck that! I don't give a fuck about Red. I'm sure who ever killed him had reason. Now I had beef with Los and all that but I didn't kill him."

"I know you didn't kill him because I killed the niggas that did that a long time ago. But did you call it?"

"What?"

"Mutha-fucka, did you call the hit on Los?"

"No. I figured out that Joe did that shit and I was happy about it. I wished I had thought of the shit first. You know I hated that nigga Los. I went to him years ago about collaborating our efforts. Since I'm the biggest on my end and he was the largest nigga on his end. We could've made millions."

"So he turned you down?"

"Yeah he did. I dropped the shit after that. When I confronted Joe about his dirt he was ready to make a deal. I told him that I would work with him if..."

"If what, nigga?" Ray needs this story to come to a close.

"If he got rid of you." Ethan stares into Kamille's eyes. "There's no need for a loud mouthed bitch to be around when we could have the shit under control."

"Is that right?" Kamille gets up from her seat. "Come here, Ethan." She's standing near the edge of the roof thirty-two stories high looking out on the city of Atlanta. Ethan is hesitant to approach but knows that he doesn't have a choice. "Everybody wanted Los' spot. Niggas killing, stealing and cheating just to be able to run shit. But the thing is, most niggas can't do what Los did. They couldn't have taught me the things that he taught me. He showed me life in a whole new light. No fears, no regrets, just live and maybe you die a respectable death. To me he did that. He died over his empire, over not letting mutha-fuckas like you take his shit. See he knew that you and even Joe, were greedy niggas and if he let you into his shit, it would soon fail. He raised me, E. I'll admit that there's a lot of shit I fucked up on, like trusting mutha-fuckas, but I've learned a lot during this process. I found a man that can take care of me. He respects me and my hustle. Your father tried to kill my mother over twenty years ago. I was there when she took his life for brutally rapping her. The look in your father's eyes reminds me of the look in your eyes right now. He knew that he was about to die and I know you know the same. So tell me E, how will your death be?"

"Fuck you, Kami! I put my blood and sweat into this shit." Kamille grabs Ethan by the back of his shirt and pushes him off the edge of the roof. His screams call out to her as she and Ray watch his body fall through the night air and splatter all over Peachtree Street.

"I thought I was going to kill the nigga." Ray is a little upset that he didn't get the chance to do the honors.

"I couldn't resist, baby. You can get the next one I promise."

"That's fucked up. I'm standing here itching like a damn junky to put a hole in his head and you push the mutha-fucka off the damn roof. Bullshit!"

"Who is it?" Natacha goes to the front door but doesn't get an answer. She looks through the peephole but can't see anyone. She grabs her Beretta off the end table and flings the door open.

Kamille steps out in full view. "Damn, what's up chick? Don't shot me."

"What the fuck?! Oh shit!" Natacha's heart hits the floor. She stands there staring at Kamille with her mouth covered.

"What's up, boo?"

"What happened? What's up? What are you doing here?"

"Slow down." Just then Ray and Tashjma come walking up the driveway. "Can we come in?"

"Yeah, bitch."

They all sit in the living room with all eyes on Natacha.

"So who's gon' tell me?" She looks at Ace with an angry smirk.

"I couldn't tell you, Ma'. I wanted to though, bad." He got up and sat next to her.

"No one could know, Natacha." Kamille assures.

"So what happened?"

"Shit is taken care of."

"What about Joe?"

"There is no more Joe, Ethan or Bridge."

"What about Ronni?"

"What about her?"

"You think we need to get one of our folks in lock up to take care of her?" "Ronni ain't got the balls to fuck with either one of us. Plus she's probably gonna get life for killing Felix."

"I guess you're right. So what? You're 'out'?"

"Hell yeah. I'm moving some damn where and chillin' the fuck out."

"What about you Ray?" Natacha glances over at her new brother-in-law.

"We goin' together."

"What about me?" Natacha asks Kamille.

"What about you? Ain't shit changed."

"We goin' too, Ace?" Natacha gives her sexy man a sexy smile.

"Hell yeah."

Natacha jumps in her seat like a schoolgirl. "Hell yeah, my bitch is back. I knew you wasn't dead." They all laugh. "And look at Ms. Tashjma." Tashjma smiles and holds her head down ashamed of the scares that still show on her face.

"I made it too." She shyly gloats.

"Hold your head up, Tashjma." Kamille orders.

"They don't look that bad." Natacha consoles her niece.

"It's alright. 'Cause first thing Monday morning I'm making an appointment with Dr. Phillips."

"Dr. Phillips?" Tashjma questions.

"She's a plastic surgeon. One of the best African-American plastic surgeons in the world.

How long did you think I'd let you walk around like that?"

"I should know better."

"You got the check yet, Natacha?" Kamille asks.

"What check?"

"The insurance check?"

"I don't know what you're talking about." They laugh.

"Chick, come up off the bread."

"Yeah I got it. I couldn't spend any of it anyway without my girl." She begins to cry. Ace gets up so that Kamille can take his place next to her friend and they embrace in laughter and tears. "But fo' real Kami, I ain't stayin' in Georgia if you ain't."

"That's cool. Where you want to go?"

"Some where cold."

"Really?"

"Yeah, like New York."

"Hell naw." Ray and Ace say in unison.

"Okay, damn, New York is out."

"We'll find somewhere. I see y'all been kickin' it hard." Kamille is referring to Natacha and Ace.

"Hell yeah, I had to call his lying ass for comfort." Natacha is jokingly referring to Ace keeping Kamille still being alive from her. "I'm glad I did though."

"Me too." Ace winks at her. "So Ray I guess this means that you've made up your mind."

"Yeah I have." Ray states as he caresses Kamille's thigh.

"Made up your mind about what?" Natacha asks, still feeling a little left out.

"He's leaving the game too." Kamille answers.

"What about Victoria?" Natacha asks a serious and fair question.

"Forgive and forget, right? I'm moving on. She's my mother and I accept her back into my life. She should be here in a minute."

"That sounds good to me."

"All I know right now is that I'm happy; happy and drama free."

Kamille sleeps in the car on the drive to Miami. Victoria needs to head down there and tie up some business before they all relocate to another state. Kamille is met by her younger self again. The young Kamille stands in a pure white dress that sways in cool air wrapped in pink, red and white rose peddles. *"You can leave me know."* The girl speaks as Kamille stands before her in her current state.

"I don't want to let you go."

"I can sleep now. Mommy's back and all is well with me now."

"I guess I have to let you go and move on."

"It's going to be okay. I'm happy now." Kamille leans down to kiss the seven year old girl that held her captive for so long. She realizes that she couldn't let go of the pain from her past while holding on to it. She watches as her younger self disappears into magnificent light. She feels someone grab her hand and turns to see Ray waiting for her. She grabs his hand and holds it tight as they walk away. *"You did good, Kami."* A voice states from behind her. She turns to see Carlos standing as a silhouette. Ray turns to see him as well. Carlos nods and smiles at them both as he turns to walk away.

16

THE NIGHT KAMILLE DIED

RAY ANSWERS HIS CELL PHONE AS HE PULLS IN A GAS STATION TO TURN AROUND, REMEMBERING THAT HE LEFT HIS KEY.

"*Yo ma' I left that key, I'm on the way back now.*" Nothing. "Hello."

He can hear conversation going on in the background

"Nigga, you betta be ready." Kamille is speaking.

"*Ready for what, baby?*"

"Fuck you, nigga."

"*What?*" And then it hit him that Kamille wasn't speaking to him. Ray pushed on the gas, knowing that it will take him about fifteen minutes to get back to the house.

"*Why in the fuck did you kill Los?*" Kamille again.

"Oh shit." Ray thought out loud.

Ray arrived at the house with it ablaze. Mrs. Fletcher was lying in the rear of the house in the yard. He fought through smoke, fire and falling debris to get to his woman. He found Kamille lying in the hallway face down, but breathing. Pulling her over his shoulder he noticed another female strapped to a chair. As he got closer he saw that it was Tashjma. Ray laid Kamille down and un-strapped Tashjma as much as he could, then pulling her onto his back, reaching down and pulling Kamille back on his shoulders, he fled from the burning house with both in tow.

Ray thought about little Mrs. Fletcher and shook his head as he went back to the burning house and pulled her body inside. He felt bad that she had no family to miss her, but satisfied that she probably didn't suffer.

He drove a little over an hour to a small town in Georgia, where he knew a doctor that would check out Kamille and Tashjma as a favor. When he got them to the doc's house and he began to strip Kamille down, in plain view was her bulletproof vest. Ray almost shed a tear at how smart his new woman was.

After Kamille woke up and Tashjma was okay to travel, they took a road trip to South Carolina and hid out there until Kamille was ready to take her revenge.

Coming Soon